A King Production presents...

All I See Is The Money...

A Novel

JOY DEJA KING

This novel is a work of fiction. Any references to real people, events, establishments, or locales are intended only to give the fiction a sense of reality and authenticity. Other names, characters, and incidents occurring in the work are either the product of the author's imagination or are used fictitiously, as those fictionalized events and incidents that involve real persons. Any character that happens to share the name of a person who is an acquaintance of the author, past or present, is purely coincidental and is in no way intended to be an actual account involving that person.

Cover concept by Joy Deja King
Cover model: Joy Deja King
Library of Congress Cataloging-in-Publication Data;

A King Production
Female Hustler Part 6/by Joy Deja King

For complete Library of Congress Copyright info visit;

www.joydejaking.com
Twitter: @joydejaking

A King Production
P.O. Box 912, Collierville, TN 38027

A King Production and the above portrayal logo are trademarks of A King Production LLC.

Copyright © 2022 by A King Production LLC. All rights reserved. No part of this book may be reproduced in any form without the permission from the publisher, except by reviewer who may quote brief passage to be printed in a newspaper or magazine.

This Book is Dedicated To My:

Family, Readers, and Supporters.
I LOVE you guys so much. Please believe that!!

—Joy Deja King

"Before You Embark On A Journey Of Revenge, Dig Two Graves..."

~Confucius~

Chapter One

Reset The Night

The breeze from the Caribbean sea and the Atlantic Ocean combined with the muggy Miami summer weather, produced thundershowers and winds that rustled up the swaying trees. Huge dark ominous clouds enveloped the skies and torrential rains were unleashed, making the night eerie. The noise from the blustering wind and lightning, seemed like a ghost stretching out his arms to Justina. She felt a chill rise up her spine, and her throat tightened. There was a low and continuous rumbling that slowly increased. Justina went cold with horror, as the storm was beginning to sweep her off the terrace but instead of seeking refuge, she stayed, staring off into the darkness.

"Justina! What tha fuck are you doin' out here!" Desmond barked, lifting her soaking wet body up from the terrace and bringing her inside the house. "I go out for fuckin' thirty minutes and this is what you do!" He continued to yell, shutting the double French doors, before wrapping the fur throw blanket around his wife.

"I thought I heard our son crying out for me. I was out there trying to save him." Justina explained, with a distant stare plastered on her face.

"How many of these pills have you taken?" Desmond asked, picking up the prescription bottle off the table. "You can't keep doing this, Justina," he shook his head with frustration. "No more pills!"

"But they're helping me."

"Helping you what...lose yo' fuckin' mind! You sound crazy!" Desmond screamed, tossing the pills in the trash.

"No! Numb the pain. I want my baby back," Justina cried. "I know you blame me for losing him."

"I just don't understand, how you didn't hear someone come into this house and take our son," Desmond fumed.

"I was so tired. I fell asleep...I'm so sorry," Justina mumbled through tears. "I already hate myself. I can't take you hating me too. I need you, Desmond."

"No, you need these pills," Desmond spit to a distraught Justina before storming off.

Justina wanted to stop Desmond from walking away but when she opened her mouth, no words came out, as if in a shock-still daze. Since the night of their son's kidnapping, Justina had become a pill popping, frazzled, borderline drunk. She was flooded with guilt. She couldn't shake something she'd read many years ago; Karma was like a rubber band. You can only stretch it so far, before it comes back and smacks you in the face. Justina believed she was now suffering the ultimate punishment, for all her sins.

"Aaliyah, I'm going out to get some things for the baby. Would you like for me to bring you anything back?"

"No, I'm good Lorita."

"Okay but call me if you change your mind," she said, leaving out.

"Will do!" Aaliyah called out, cradling Justina's son, like he was her own. "Such a beautiful baby boy," she smiled, imagining how her son with Dale would've looked, if he hadn't died before even taking his first breath.

While Aaliyah sat in the rocking chair, staring out the huge bay window, she relished at how perfectly her plan came together. In the beginning, it felt like a long, tedious journey. But with the ending results, it was all worthwhile.

Once being released from the hospital and leaving Miami, to stay with her parents at their estate in New Jersey, the heartbreak of losing her husband and baby, was excruciating for Aaliyah. She could barely get out of bed, let alone leave the house. At her lowest point, there were moments when she even begged God, to put her out of her misery and let her go be with the love of her life and unborn child. Then one morning, Aaliyah caught a reflection of herself in the bathroom mirror. She didn't recognize who she was. It was as if she was staring at a stranger. Aaliyah was desperate to find a reason to live and sweet revenge became her motivation.

Aaliyah had no idea who was responsible for Dale's death, so she decided to focus her attention on a person who was much more tangible... Justina. She blamed her former best friend, for robbing her and Dale of precious time together, by purposely letting him find out, her father was the one who killed his brother Emory. Her wedding day was ruined and it could've ended a lot worse, if Desmond hadn't taken the bullet for Supreme. Aaliyah found it ironic, the man who saved her father's life, ended up being Justina's husband. *How did that scheming heifa, end up with the fairytale life that should've been mine*, she thought, shaking her head.

Aaliyah couldn't bring back her husband or baby but she was determined to make sure, Justina didn't have her happy ending either. That unwavering goal, was the spark she needed, to ditch her gloom and doom mood, for the perfect takedown of Justina's happy home. All Aaliyah needed was the right inside person and who better than the nanny. Lorita had played her role flawlessly and everything was coming together just how she envisioned.

"Fuck, that's my mother calling again." Aaliyah rolled her eyes, ready to send Precious straight to voicemail but thought better of it and answered, since the baby had fallen asleep. "Hello."

"Finally! I can't believe you answered. I was beginning to think you were ignoring my calls," Precious complained.

"Now mother, why would I do that," Aaliyah said cheerfully. "I always love talking to you but I've started taking some classes and by the time I'm done, I then go to the gym, and afterwards, I'm completely exhausted," she explained.

"You started taking classes...I had no idea. That's wonderful, Aaliyah. What sort of classes are you taking?" Precious asked.

"Just different things." Aaliyah was intentionally being vague. "You know, to keep me busy and not thinking about Dale and our child so much."

"Oh, baby girl, I think that's wonderful.

I'm so proud of you for making an effort, to do something positive, to work through your pain. It's important you find constructive ways to deal with your loss."

"You're absolutely right and that's exactly what I'm doing." Aaliyah smiled, looking down at Justina's baby. "This new direction I'm taking with my life, has completely changed my outlook. The healing has truly begun."

"I've been praying so hard for this to happen and finally, my prayers have been answered. I truly love you with all my heart, Aaliyah."

"And I love you too," she replied sweetly.

"Listen, I'm headed to the city. Why don't I come over. We can order food and watch some of our favorite movies. Or, we can go out and eat at that restaurant you love so much on the Upper West Side," Precious suggested.

"Mom, I would love to but I'm already running late for my class," Aaliyah lied and said.

"Why don't we go out to eat after your class. I'm sure you'll be hungry."

"I wish but we're having a guest speaker and then a Q&A afterwards, so I won't be home until really late. But I promise, we'll get together soon," Aaliyah said, trying to rush her mother off the phone.

"Okay! I'ma hold you to that promise, Aaliyah."

"Please do…love you!"

"Love you too. I'll talk…hello?" Precious looked at her phone, realizing Aaliyah had already hung up. "I guess she really was running late," Precious mumbled, thinking something felt peculiar with how her daughter was acting. Instead of dwelling on it, she dismissed her misgivings. Precious wanted to celebrate the fact, for the first time, Aaliyah didn't sound miserable but instead was making plans with her life and seemed optimistic about her future.

Chapter Two

Unhinged

"Spending these last few weeks with you, have been amazing," Angel gushed, lathering her husband's chest with body wash, while he sat on the bench in their marble clad shower.

"Yo, it's been heaven," Darien agreed, as the steaming hot water splashed against his and Angel's skin."We needed this time together, with all the craziness that's been going down over the past months."

"Who you telling. Honestly, I'm wishing I've been stuck in a bad dream and any minute, I'll wake up realizing none of it happened, except the part where Taren is dead," Angel said. "I was actually thinking about going to New York to visit Aaliyah. She's been sounding more like herself lately but I know losing the baby and Dale is still taking its toll on her spirit."

"I think it'd be good for you to go see your sister. I only met Dale a couple times but he seemed like a decent dude. For him to get murdered like that, is fucked up," Darien said, shaking his head. "Man, you have to appreciate each day, especially with the ones you love," he continued, placing his hand on Angel's wrist. "I hope you know, how blessed I feel to have you."

Darien pulled Angel down and kissed her soft lips, which immediately made his dick rock hard. He wrapped his arms around her waist, pulling her closer, as her naked body pressed against his. He swiped his tongue across her bottom lip. She straddled her husband, who was still sitting on the bench. The water cascaded down Angel's back as she took a deep breath, pleasurably taking in every inch of his manhood. She couldn't control her cries of pleasure. She called out her husband's name which made Darien even more aroused, causing each thrust to go deeper and deeper. He wasn't sure if it was due to the running water from the shower but to him, Angel's pussy sounded like waves hitting, very soothing.

They took turns biting and kissing each other's neck. The pounding became harder and more intense and Angel felt l a tingle running through her entire body. Darien could feel her pussy tighten up around his dick and the wetness increased as her juices dripped down. Her screams of pleasure now turned into a soft cry. Moments later, Angel could feel the warmth of her husband's cum inside her, oozing out as he continued to slowly stroke, giving his wife every bit he had left. In that moment, for them, it was the best feeling in the world.

"Damn, I love you." Dariensaid, sprinkling kisses on his wife's shoulder.

"I love you too," Angel whispered.

Angel and Darien eventually took their love session into the bedroom, before falling asleep in each other's arms. Passionate sex makes for the best sleep, so it was easy for Angel to ignore the text messages she was receiving. But being bombarded with phone calls wasn't quite as easy, although she tried.

"Hello." Angel finally answered still half asleep.

"It took me calling you a hundred times but thank goodness you answered!" Elsa screamed into the phone.

"Why are you shouting in my ear and why are you interrupting me on my last day off? We just got back in town yesterday and I'm not due into the office until tomorrow!" Angel snapped.

"You said to call if there was an extreme emergency. You need to get to the office ASAP!"

"Fuck! I'm on the way," Angel mumbled. "So much for one more day of peace," she sighed tossing down her phone.

"Detective Torres, come in," Desmond said, holding the door open. "Do you have any news for us?"

"Not yet but I do have some questions. Is your wife home?" the detective asked.

"Yes, she's upstairs. Justina!" Desmond called out, walking up the stairs. Right when he was about to call her name again, he saw his wife coming down the hallway.

"I heard the doorbell. Did they find our son?" Justina had a faraway gaze in her eyes. "Is our baby finally home?"

"No. Detective Torres is here. He has some questions for us." Desmond took Justina's hand and led her down the stairs. He barely recognized the woman he'd fallen madly in love with less than a year ago. It was as if after their son had been kidnapped, the life was sucked out of her.

"What can we do for you detective?" Justina's voice was barely audible.

"I wanted to confirm the name of your son's nanny. I wrote down," he paused for a second, looking down at a notepad he was holding although he remembered the name. "Fiorella Perez. Are you sure that's her name?"

"Of course I'm sure," Justina confirmed.

"Why, is there a problem with the name?" Desmond questioned with annoyance.

"There's a serious problem. This Fiorella Perez woman doesn't seem to exist?" Detective Torres informed the couple, walking closer to Justina.

"You must be mistaken," Justin mumbled.

"No, I'm not. I tried calling the number you gave me too and it's not in service. I also went to the address you gave me for Ms. Perez and no one by that name has ever lived there. I decided to pay a visit to the nanny agency you said referred you to Ms. Perez and no one has heard of her either."

"I don't understand." Justina shook her head, taken aback by what the detective was saying.

"Mrs. Blackwell, are you sure someone came into your home and took your son? It can be difficult for new mothers to adjust. Some even snap. Is that what happened to you, the night your baby went missing?"

"Get the fuck out my house!" Desmond barked. "How dare you accuse my wife of some bullshit like that. What tha fuck is wrong wit' you!"

"Sir, I'm going to need you to calm down. I'm simply trying to do my job and find out what happened to your son. You weren't even in town when he went missing. You also told me on my previous visit here, that it was your wife who hired the nanny and you only met her a few times. It doesn't seem strange to you, this Fiorella woman doesn't exist, there is no trace of anyone besides your wife being in the home on the night of your child's disappearance, there was no forcible entry and the security footage from the night in question, has somehow vanished?"

"I told you, Fiorella stopped by briefly the night my son went missing. She was going to visit her family and wanted to see Desi before she left. She can vouch for me that he was here, in his crib. I didn't do anything to my baby. He was safe!" Justina implored.

"The problem is, Fiorella Perez seems to be a figment of your imagination, Mrs. Blackwell," Detective Torres stated candidly.

"If you have any further questions for my wife, you can speak to our attorney. But unless you want me to file a lawsuit against you and the MPD, I advise you, to do your job and find the person responsible for kidnapping our son and stop harassing my wife. Now get out of my house...now!" Desmond shouted, holding the door open before slamming it close, almost hitting the detective as he walked out. "How dare that muthafucker accuse you of some shit like that," Desmond fumed pouring himself a drink.

"What if he's right. What if I did hurt Desi and I don't remember." Justina clutched her bathrobe, falling down on the couch.

"Don't do this!" Desmond slammed his glass down on top of the bar. "There is no way you would hurt our son."

"Then what happened to him and how in the hell does Fiorella not exist?! You met her! I'm not crazy!"

"Baby, of course I met her." Desmond assured Justina, cupping her face in his hand. "And no, you're not crazy. Did you sleep at all last night?" he asked with concern, observing the dark circles under her eyes.

"No!" Justina snapped. "I haven't slept in days. Not since you threw away my pills." Justina stood up, releasing herself from her husband's grasp. "But of course you wouldn't notice because instead of being here with me, you're at that fuckin' club!"

"Justina, I'm working."

"How can you work knowing our child is missing or could even be dead?" she exclaimed.

"Don't say that!" Desmond hollered. "Our son is not dead! And I have to work because if I stay in this house wit' you, I'd..." His voice faded off.

"You'd what? Say it, Desmond. You'd wanna kill me. You can't stand looking at me or even touching me. So, of course you would rather go to work, then stay here and grieve with me." Justina yelled.

Desmond who was rarely, if ever at a loss for words, was speechless. He didn't want to kill his wife but he'd be lying, if he didn't admit, he felt some sort of resentment towards her. He didn't believe for a second, the detective's theory that Justina had something to do with their son's disappearance but it did bother him, his wife slept through the entire ordeal. Not only that, the way Justina seemed to crumble in the aftermath, made things even worse. Besides her beauty, one of the reasons Desmond was so drawn to his wife, was because of her fiery personality and resilience. Seeing her so fragile, he wasn't sure what to do.

"Justina, you're my wife and I love you but I feel helpless. I'm used to being in control and finding solutions but for the first time in my adult life, I have none. I can't find our son and I can't seem to help you. It's like I lost both of you the night he was kidnapped," Desmond stated.

"If you really want to help me, you'll get my prescription refilled, so I can get some sleep. And don't fuckin' wake me up, until you find our baby."

With those words, Justina headed back upstairs, leaving Desmond feeling somewhat relieved. For the first time since their son was kidnapped, he was able to see a glimpse of the bitchy Justina, that he adored.

Chapter Three

Things Ain't The Same

"Elsa, this better be good," Angel huffed, approaching her desk. "I was lying in bed with my husband. Enjoying our last day together before coming back to work and then you call. What is so urgent, you had to tell me in person, instead of over the phone?"

Elsa put her finger up, signaling to Angel she was wrapping up a phone call. "Mr. Andrews, I will look into this and get back to you as quickly as possible. Thanks so much for letting me know," she said before hanging up the phone.

"Was that Marcus Andrews you were on the phone with?" Angel questioned. Elsa nodded her head yes. "He's one of our best clients. I hope there's not a problem."

"This is more than a problem. It's more like a catastrophe." Elsa stood up and came from behind her desk.

"Spit it out, Elsa!" Angel was growing impatient.

"Only two of our girls showed up for work and met with their clients. The rest are ghost."

"Excuse me? What do you mean ghost?"

"The phones have been ringing nonstop…as you can see." Elsa scowled up her face, as the calls kept coming in. "Mr. Andrews called because Lexi was supposed to be at his hotel suite when his flight landed. She was a no show."

"Did you try calling her?"

"I started calling her this morning, to make sure she was at his hotel on time. I know how much money he spends, so of course I like to keep Mr. Andrews happy. Lexi hasn't answered my calls. I then started reaching out to some of our other girls, so they could cover for her but none of them are responding either. I don't know what is going on, Angel," Elsa said with frustration.

"Well, I'm about to fuckin' find out!" She had every single one of Angel's Girls on speed dial but their phone either went straight to voicemail, or no one picked up. "These chicks can't be serious." Angel was stunned.

"Now do you see why I called you. I mean, this can't be a coincidence right?" Elsa questioned.

"Of course this ain't no damn coincidence. But they better have a good fuckin' reason, why they ditched work, or it's gonna be a massacre up in here," Angel seethed.

"This is really nice," Precious smiled, taking a bite of her mustard glazed grilled salmon. "It was a pleasant surprise when you called, inviting me to lunch."

"What can I say...I missed my mother," Aaliyah said cheerfully, sipping her wine.

"Not as much as I've missed you. By the way, did I tell you how gorgeous you look? You're glowing!"

Precious absolutely loved the two piece, multi colored chiffon outfit Aaliyah was wearing. The set had an off shoulder green top that tied in the back with flounce sleeves. The maxi skirt had a tiered color block pattern. It looked like her daughter should be having drinks on an exotic island, instead of a high-end Manhattan restaurant.

"Yes, mother," Aaliyah grinned. "You've told me at least a handful of times."

"I can't help it. I'm loving your entire look. The high ponytail and hoop earrings, are really giving me salsa dance vibes." Mother and daughter both started laughing. "It makes my heart sing to see my beautiful daughter, laughing and smiling again. You seem genuinely happy."

"I am. This new project I'm working on, has really brought me unimaginable happiness."

"Wow! Does this project have something to do with school?" Precious asked, very intrigued.

"It's actually an outside undertaking but I'm definitely learning a lot."

"Tell me more?" Precious questioned, leaning forward.

"Not yet." Aaliyah said, coyly. "It's still in the beginning stages but once it's come full circle, I will tell you all about it," she promised.

"Can't wait! It must be pretty amazing to put such a huge smile on your face."

"Beyond amazing. It's the exact distraction I needed to start healing. Of course, there will always be a void in my heart, that nothing or no one, will be able to fill but I finally feel alive again."

"Aaliyah, I'm so proud of you." Precious reached across the table and held her daughter's hand tightly. "You are truly a survivor."

"Yes, I am," Aaliyah agreed.

"I'm excited for this new journey you're on," Precious beamed.

"So am I. Speaking of my new journey, it's going to take me around the world."

"What do you mean?" Precious let go of her daughter's hand, eyeballing her.

"This new project I'm working on, will require me to do a lot of traveling. I've always wanted to take a trip around the world and I think this is the perfect opportunity."

"You've never mentioned wanting to travel around the world. In the past, you would always make comments like it would be a waste of your time because you could get everything you needed within the fifty states, or on a private island," Precious recalled.

"That was the old Aaliyah. The new Aaliyah, views life from a much different perspective."

"I see."

"Why do you seem so disappointed? I thought you'd be thrilled, I wanted to get out and explore the world."

"I'm not disappointed. Shocked would be a better word. This all seems so sudden."

"I'm not leaving tomorrow, mother," Aaliyah giggled, trying to keep the mood upbeat. "I still have some loose ends to tie up. It won't be for another few weeks."

"Few weeks?!" Precious almost choked on her Moscato. "So soon? I was thinking more like a few months."

"Like I said, it's for a new project I'm working on and it requires me to do some traveling."

"How long will you be gone?"

"I'm not sure yet but stop worrying. I'll be calling you and we can facetime. We'll be in touch frequently." Aaliyah reassured her mother.

"Why does this feel so final? You almost sound like you're never come back."

"OMG! Mother, stop being so dramatic."

Aaliyah playfully hit Precious's arm.

"I thought that was the two of you, I saw when I came in."

"Lorenzo, it's good to see you," Precious looked up and said.

"It's good to see you too. How are you both doing?" he asked, continuing to look at Precious, before glancing over at Aaliyah, who was replying to a text message.

"I'm doing great and you?" Precious smiled.

Before he could respond, Aaliyah interrupted. "Lorenzo, it's nice seeing you and you're looking as handsome as ever. I hate to say hi and bye but I have to go."

"But we just ordered our dessert. You can't leave now," Precious protested.

"I know but I got a text from the person I'm working with on my project. An emergency came up and I have to go," Aaliyah said, grabbing her purse. "Lorenzo, sit down. You can have my dessert. It's super yummy!" Aaliyah gave her mother a quick kiss goodbye.

"Please, sit down...I mean if you don't mind. I really do hate eating alone," Precious said, watching her daughter rush off.

"I don't mind," Lorenzo said, taking a seat.

"The way Aaliyah ran outta here, must be some project she's working on," he remarked.

"How can someone seem so together, yet everything feels off?" Precious wanted to know.

"I'm assuming you're speaking about your daughter."

"Yes but I'm just being paranoid," Precious shook her head.

"You're a lot of things but paranoid isn't one of them," Lorenzo countered. "I know you very well, Precious. If something seems off to you, then more than likely it is. You have many excellent traits and your great intuition is one of them. It's always been on point."

"You would know." Precious gave a sly smile. "My instincts did tell me, your heart still belonged to Dior, even when we were together and I was right."

"True but your heart also still belonged to Supreme. But don't ever doubt my heart belonging to Dior, in any way, diminished how I felt about you."

"Oh, I never doubted that for a second." Precious admitted with ease.

"Confidence, is another trait you never lacked," Lorenzo chuckled.

"True." Precious laughed. "But seriously, I know what we shared was real. I also know, we both ended up with who, we're supposed to be with."

"I agree but our relationship sure did ruffle a lot of feathers." Lorenzo shook his head, thinking about all the drama it caused.

"Ruffled a lot of feathers is an understatement. Our relationship was the catalyst, for Chantal almost ruining Aaliyah's life and destroying my marriage. Those were some very dark times. To this day, it amazes me, you all are not fans of one another but still manage to conduct business with each other," Precious proclaimed.

"Two reasons…money and Genesis. Of course Supreme and T-Roc have their own paper and business entities separate from us but they have mad love and respect for Genesis. We all do. He's the core of the group. Trust me, it does get intense sometimes because the dislike is real," Lorenzo laughed. "But we do our best, to put it aside for the greater good."

"You know how fond I am of Genesis, so it makes sense," Precious agreed.

"I know what you're doing right now," Lorenzo said, eyeing Precious keenly.

"What are you talking about?"

"Didn't we already establish that I know you very well."

"Yes...and?" Precious shrugged.

"I know you're trying to divert the conversation, to keep from talking about what's really bothering you."

"Which is?"

"I'm about one hundred percent positive it's Aaliyah. I know she's had a rough time these past few months but she seems to be in a good place. On the flipside, a mother's intuition is almost never wrong, when it comes to her child. So, what's bothering you?"

"I'm sure this will sound crazy but she seems to be in a, too good of a place. It's almost like overnight, Aaliyah went from not wanting to get out of bed, to moving out and getting her own place. Like how does one go from being severely depressed, to extra bubbly and happy? And although she's sharing what's going on in her life with me, she's also become super secretive. I know my thoughts seem to be scattered and a bit contradictory but..."

"No it doesn't," Lorenzo stated, cutting Precious off. "It's called peeping game. It sounds like your daughter is trying to run it on you and you're not having it."

"But there's no proof...no evidence she's up to anything but I can't shake the feeling. It's driving me crazy. Then I feel guilty, for thinking the worse of my own child. The thing is, I know my daughter, probably even better than I know myself. Something is very wrong with this picture, Aaliyah continues to paint so carefully."

"Then sit back and keep your eyes open. Trust me, when you seek the truth, it always comes to you. Just be prepared for whatever it brings because most of the time, it ain't nothing nice."

"You're right and that's what I'm so afraid of," she admitted. "I'm not ready for the storm." Precious pushed away the dessert she hadn't taken one bite of. Her appetite was now nonexistent and her heart was heavy, but she knew Lorenzo was speaking the truth. She had to be prepared, because she was willing to walk through fire to protect her daughter. And Precious had a feeling, Aaliyah would need her now more than ever.

Chapter Four

Don't Judge Me

Justina spent her days in a self-induced coma, with a cocktail of pills and booze. She was relieved Desmond didn't put up a fight, about getting her prescription refilled. She figured her husband realized, he was gambling with her sanity, if she continued being sleep deprived. As Justina was closing her eyes for some more shuteye, she heard the doorbell ring. At first, she chose to ignore it but when it persisted, she remembered the new security system Desmond had installed. She could see who was at the door from the comforter of her bed.

"If this isn't news about my baby, please go away," she groaned, sliding over to the other side of the bed to view the security camera. "Omigosh!" Justina jumped out of bed in disbelief and ran to open the door.

"Are you gonna stand there, or give your father a hug?" T-Roc said, reaching out to Justina.

"Daddy, I'm so happy to see you." Justina fell into her father's arms, welcoming his embrace. "I can't believe you're here," she cried.

"Of course I'm here. You're my baby girl. I'm always with you, even when you don't know it," he said holding her tightly.

Once they were inside the house, T-Roc and Justina sat on the couch in silence for a few minutes, as she continued sobbing in her father's arms. She didn't realize just how much she needed her dad's love and support, until that very moment.

"Do the police have any leads?" T-Roc asked Justina, once she seemed calm.

"No. The main detective working the case,

actually accused me of harming my own child," Justina revealed, becoming angry thinking about it.

"What?! Why would he even think something so crazy?"

"When Desi was first kidnapped, they asked if anyone had access to our home and interaction with our son. So of course, I told them about his nanny Fiorella. Come to find out, this Fiorella chick doesn't exist. Obviously, she gave me a fake name, fake everything."

"Then this Fiorella woman must be the one who kidnapped my grandson." T-Roc stated.

"Exactly! But this stupid detective seems to think, she's some make believe nanny I created to cover up my crime," Justina scoffed. "The audacity of that man."

"I hope you told him to get the hell out of your house!" T-Roc fumed.

"No but Desmond did. He was furious."

"As he shoulda been! The nerve of that man. With all you've been through, to then accuse you of something so heinous. I'm sorry you had to deal with that, Justina," T-Roc said, hugging his daughter again.

"Daddy, this pain I'm feeling...it's almost

unbearable," she professed, pulling away.

"That's natural. Your child was taken away from you, Justina. I'm still having a hard time wrapping my head around this bullshit. I don't know how you're handling all this...and where is your husband? He should be here with you."

"Desmond's at work," Justina said, keeping her distance.

"I hope you mean, out working this fuckin' case, trying to find his son!" T-Roc barked.

"He has hired some private investigators to handle the case but he's working at one of his clubs right now."

"He should be here with you."

"Initially I felt the same way but now, I think it's better he's at work. There's nothing he can do for me here. All I want to do is sleep anyway. It's the only time I feel like, I don't want to die," Justina's voice cracked as she tried to hold back her tears.

"Baby girl." T-Roc walked closer to his daughter. Refusing to allow her, to put this space between them."I know the pain seems unbearable but you gotta fight against it. Think of your son and how much he'll need you, once he comes home."

"What if doesn't come home."

"You can't think like that! Do you understand me!" T-Roc squeezed Justina's arms, as if trying to release some of his strength into her. This isn't the time to be weak. Your son needs you. That's the only thing you need to be focusing on."

"I'm trying but it's so hard."

"Then try harder," he demanded. "I can clean up your messes but I can't make you be a warrior. That has to come from within you." T-Roc's blood was boiling. His frustration continued to build, feeling he wasn't reaching his daughter. "My lovely, Justina. You got all of your mother's beauty but you also inherited so many of her flaws and unfortunately, some of mine. But one thing I'm not, is weak."

"I hate seeing that look of disappointment in your eyes. That's why I didn't want you coming here." Justina turned away, so she wouldn't have to face her father. "I didn't want you to see me like this."

"I'm your father. No matter how I feel, I will always be here for you. And it's not disappointment you see in my eyes, it's concern."

"You say that but I remember when I was at that facility in California. You never wanted to come visit me. You thought I was a failure. After the situation with Amir, Aaliyah, the trial and what mother did, I couldn't pull myself out of the depression I was in. You blamed me for being weak," Justina stated sadly.

"No, you're wrong. I blamed myself for not protecting you. I felt responsible. Like it was my fault, your life was spinning out of control. When you were born, you were the sweetest baby. Never cried," T-Roc said, holding his daughter's hand.

"Daddy stop." Justina pulled away again, not wanting to revisit the past.

But T-Roc persisted. He desperately wanted to reach his daughter, for them to have a breakthrough. "Growing up, you never gave us any trouble. Your brother was the rebellious one. You on the other hand would sit in your room and play with your dolls, perfectly content. Because of that, I think your mother and I neglected you in so many ways, especially emotionally. We were too busy living our lives." Guilt was gnawing at T-Roc.

"You don't have to explain yourself to me."

"Yes I do. I never felt like I've failed at anything in my life but I failed you. I'm a flawed and selfish man, Justina. But God as my witness, I would give my life for you. I love you more than anything in this world and I've never seen you as a failure...never."

Justina was looking away from her father but turned to face him with sorrow in her eyes. "You wouldn't be saying these things to me if you knew the truth. I'm not the sweet little girl, sitting in my room, playing with dolls anymore. If you knew all the bad things I've done, I would be a failure to you." Justina put her head down and began to sob. "Daddy, I've done some terrible things. I think losing my beautiful baby boy, is Karma serving me, exactly what I deserve."

Justina was on the verge, of spilling all of her darkest secrets to her father but stopped herself, before saying another word. She wanted to confess her sins but the fear of losing his love, made her hold back. She battled with her conscious while locking eyes with him. As if reading her mind, T-Roc walked over to his daughter and held her tightly. He knew Justina didn't need to be judged right now, she needed the love of her father.

Female Hustler Part 6

"You all wait right here for me," Angel told two of Darien's security guards, when they arrived at Buttonwood Lane, an upscale Miami suburb. "If I'm not out in five minutes, then you know what to do."

"Are you sure you don't want us to come with you?" Benito asked, not wanting anything to happen to his boss's wife.

"I got this," Angel said, flashing the Glock she kept in her purse. "But you can go ahead and set your timer for those five minutes." Angel stepped out of the SUV and headed towards the contemporary waterfront home. She rang the doorbell and then banged on the front door, wanting to make her presence known. It took a minute but someone finally came to the door.

"Hey!" A bubbly blonde answered. She was wearing a itty bitty pink bikini and Angel noticed a trace of white powder on her nostril.

"Hi. I'm Angel. I'm here to see Lexi."

"Who?" she questioned, looking genuinely perplexed by the name.

"She's a working girl like you," Angel stated,

brushing past the woman and coming into the house. She glanced around, at the dramatic ceiling heights with walls of glass.

"You can't come in here!" The high as a kite blonde protested.

"You're too late...I'm already in here. Excuse me, I have an idea where Lexi is," Angel scoffed, dismissing the girl. She followed the loud music which led her to the outdoor amenities. Cardi B's Money Bag, was blaring from the speakers, as the small group was having their own private party. There was a dozen or so, bikini clad women, entertaining a few men. Angel spotted Lexi, in the infinity edge swimming pool, giving one of the men, a blowjob. Everyone was too preoccupied with liquor, drugs, or some form of sex act, to even notice, or care, Angel was an uninvited guest.

Angel knelt down at the side of the pool, where Lexi was finishing up the last of her licking and sucking. The man was grunting loudly and then started pressing down on the back of her neck, gripping it tighter, right before exploding his seeds in Lexi's mouth.

"You blew off one of my biggest clients, so you could come here and act like a groupie hoe, in some bootleg looking music video," Angel snapped. She shocked the fuck out of Lexi so bad, that she spit out the man's cum, barely missing his face.

"What tha fuck!" He jumped, turning around to see who was sabotaging his high.

"Angel, what are you doing here?!" The embarrassment of it all, was plastered across Lexi's face.

"The question is…what the fuck are you doing here?"

"I'm working," she stuttered.

"Working where? I know not fuckin' here!" Angel stood up, looking down on Lexi. "Get yo' shit and let's go!" Angel demanded.

"She ain't goin' nowhere. We hired her for the whole fuckin' day," the man popped, finally covering up his now limp dick.

"Angel, I can explain," Lexi mumbled, getting out of the pool.

"Where you goin'?!" the man shouted. He followed Lexi out the pool and grabbed her wrist. "I ain't done wit' you. We paid for you and the rest of these broads to be here until we done wit' you and we ain't done yet!"

Angel cut her eyes at the man and was ready

to smack the shit out of Lexi, for even dealing with this lowlife. "Dude, you need to step back and get yo' hands off of her," Angel popped.

"Who tha fuck you think you talkin' to!" He let go of Lexi's wrist and stepped to Angel with his nose flaring.

"Nigga, I'm talking to you." Angel stated calmly. He started to raise his hand and she immediately pulled out her Glock. "This ain't fo' show. I will use this muthafucka on you." She made clear.

The man backed up and then hollered for his cronies. But before they could even think about breaking bad, the goons Angel made sure to bring with her, appeared right on time.

"Benito, over here!" Angel waved her hand at them, before focusing her attention back on Lexi.

"Angel, I'm sorry."

"Save your apology, Lexi. I put you on and even advanced you money because you couldn't pay yo' fuckin' rent and this is how you do me. Where's the fuckin' loyalty. Not here," Angel shook her head. "Enough of that for now...you comin' wit' me. I wanna know who the fuck hired you for this gig and where the rest of the disloyal chicks who bailed on me are," Angel fussed.

"Okay, let me get my stuff," Lexi agreed, keeping her head down.

"I'm gettin' a fuckin' refund!" The man shouted as Lexi and Angel walked off.

Chapter Five

Fail You Never Again

"What has my beautiful wife in such deep thought?" Supreme whispered in Precious's ear, as he walked up from behind and wrapped his arms around her waist. She was standing quietly on the bedroom terrace, staring out at the opulent waterfall.

"What isn't on my mind," she said, turning to give her husband a kiss. "I'm so happy, Genesis finally has his daughter back but I'm worried about Skylar. The longer she remains in a coma, the odds of her waking up aren't good."

"I know but all we can do is keep her in our prayers. She took a bullet to protect her daughter. I have a feeling God got her back," Supreme smiled. "I think she'll pull through."

"Thank you for saying that. I know some people would rather she stay in a coma," Precious frowned. "But I have a lot of love for Skylar and I know how much she loves Genevieve."

"I'll be the first to admit, Skylar makes things more complicated. Genesis is married to Talisa and she's the woman he wants to spend the rest of his life with. Skylar is the mother of his child and he loves her too. But Genesis is a good man and I have no doubt it will all work out," Supreme said, kissing Precious on the neck.

"You can't kiss on me like that, when you're about to leave," Precious sighed, closing her eyes loving the touch of Supreme's lips on her skin.

"No worries, I won't be gone long. I was thinking, maybe we could go out and have a nice dinner, then come home and I could put you to bed."

"That sounds perfect. I was thinking later on

this week, maybe you, me and Aaliyah could have dinner together," Precious suggested. She was trying to find a way to bring up their daughter without sounding like she was worried.

"We can do that. I actually saw Aaliyah the other day."

"Really! Why didn't you mention it?"

"She just stopped by my office, after one of her classes. She didn't stay long."

"Oh. How did she seem to you?"

"Great. She looked happy. Our daughter is very resilient like her mother."

"Don't you think she seems too happy?" Precious questioned.

"Honestly, I was a bit surprised at how upbeat she was. But I rather her be in a positive place, than how she was, when you first brought her home from Miami. Aaliyah wouldn't even come out her room. I didn't say it then because I knew how worried you were but I was scared for our daughter. So, I'm relieved she seems optimistic about life again," Supreme admitted.

"Well, I'm still worried. Do you think Aaliyah found out who killed Dale and she's plotting some sort of revenge?"

Supreme had a grimace stare on his face.

"We don't even know who killed Dale, so how would she...where did that come from?"

"Aaliyah can be very resourceful when she wants to be. Maybe I'm reaching but something has all of a sudden brought her out of that depression she was in and it ain't no fuckin' classes."

"So plotting on the person who murdered her husband, would all of a sudden make her look and feel happy again?" Supreme side eyed his wife, not convinced with her theory. "If anything, wouldn't she be more angry," he reasoned.

"True." Precious stared back off for a second, becoming lost in the comforting sound of the waterfalls, before continuing." The day we were leaving the hospital and you were shot, is still fresh in my mind. When I thought you were dead, I wanted to die. The only reason I had to live, was because I was determined to find who shot you and make them pay. When I was plotting my revenge, never was I happy. I succumbed to anger, every single day. So you're right. This new, lively energy Aaliyah is full of, has nothing to do with plotting on the person who killed her husband but something is off."

"Are you sure you're just not being a

concerned mother," Supreme said, caressing his wife's hand.

"I wish it was only that but something has given Aaliyah a reason to live. And I have a bad feeling, nothing good is going to come from it."

"Vincent, let me give you a call back," Desmond said, hanging up the phone.

"I'm so sorry, Mr. Blackwell but he insisted I let him come in. And, I mean he is T-Roc," the newly hired and soon to be fired receptionist blushed.

"No problem. He's my father-in-law. T-Roc is always welcomed in my office," Desmond politely stated. "And you can close the door," he told the receptionist, who seemed like she didn't want to leave. "It's a pleasure to finally meet you." Desmond walked over and shook T-Roc's hand. "I'm assuming Justina knows you're in town."

"She does. I just left your house. I wanted to come here because I thought it was time, I met my daughter's husband in person. Especially since, me nor my wife got an invite to the wedding," T-Roc remarked.

"I'm glad you did. I've been looking forward to meeting you. Please sit down. Can I get you anything?" Desmond offered.

"No I'm good," T-Roc replied taking a seat.

"Like I mentioned on our phone conversation, after I married your daughter," Desmond continued. "We plan on having a much bigger wedding, with all of our family and friends. Of course those plans have now been delayed, due to the kidnapping of our son."

"It's the reason I'm here. To find out who took my grandson and why. But my question to you is, why are you here at work, instead of being home with your wife?"

"That's a fair question," Desmond acknowledged.

"I know...that's why I asked and I would appreciate you give me an answer."

Desmond wanted to select his words carefully but also be honest. He had a great deal of respect for T-Roc and it wasn't because he was famous. He admired his business savvy. T-Roc took everything he learned in the entertainment industry and meticulously built his own empire.

"As you can imagine, our son's kidnapping has taken a toll on both of us. We're dealing with it the best we can. Justina is taking pills, which causes her to sleep most of the day and night. I'm throwing myself into work. Some might disagree with how we're handling things but until you've been through it, you have no idea what you'll do. Now I understand why a lot of marriages don't survive a loss of a child," Desmond conceded.

"I appreciate your honesty, Desmond...I really do but that's why it's critical, you be there for your wife. Unless you have no interest in saving your marriage?" T-Roc questioned.

"I wouldn't have asked Justina to be my wife, if I wasn't willing to do anything to make our marriage work."

"Maybe you did then but now you've changed your mind. It does happen, especially if you learn certain things about your spouse."

"I know everything about Justina," Desmond said, making sure to put emphasis on the word everything.

"Are you sure?' T-Roc countered.

Desmond eyed T-Roc suspiciously but remained confident with his answer. "Yes...I'm positive."

"Then why didn't my daughter tell you about Nesa?"

"She did and I thought it was handled. I'ma take a wild guess and say Justina didn't tell you about her involvement with Nesa. Which means, you could've only found out one way...Nesa contacting you."

"Since we're being honest, yes she did. She threatened to expose Justina if I didn't pay her off."

"I did pay Nesa off but instead of taking my advice, she clearly got greedy."

"Pretty much, so I made sure she was taken care of permanently."

"It was you who killed Nesa?" Desmond presumed.

"Of course I didn't do it personally but I made sure it was handled. I will always do whatever necessary, to protect my family," T-Roc made clear. "I learned a long time ago, when someone tries to shake you down for money, if you give it to them, they'll keep coming back for more. Unless you don't mind being their personal ATM, then erase them for good. Nesa would've been a problem and I had no intention, of being her go to money guy."

"I feel you," Desmond nodded, shifting in his chair. "Her murder had Justina shook for a minute. She thought I did it and was worried the police would trace it back to me."

"There's no need to worry about Nesa's murder but Justina has gotten her hands dirty, in a lot of other things too."

"I know this. Your daughter confessed all her secrets to me a long time ago."

"And yet you still married her."

"I love Justina very much. She has a troubled past and can be complicated but having our son has softened her in so many ways. Almost to the point..." Desmond's voice trailed off, not completing his thought.

"To the point that she's become weak," T-Roc said it for him.

"I don't want to use the term weak but."

"But noting. That's exactly what has happened. Of course you didn't know Justina when she was a little girl and I doubt she talks about it much. But she was so shy and sweet. All she did was play with her dolls and follow around her best friend Aaliyah. Justina practically worshipped her. Aaliyah was everything she wasn't... confident, outspoken, bossy and at times, downright rude," T-Roc laughed. "I blame myself a lot for Justina's self-esteem issues. I'm guessing teaming up with Maya, was her way of finally feeling in control of something."

"Wow. I had no idea you knew about the Maya situation. Am I wrong to assume you also know about Markell?" Desmond was curious to know.

"Yeah, that one hurt. I had a lot of love for Markell. He even worked for me at one time." T-Roc stood up, shaking his head. "I would've never thought Justina was capable of such deception."

"Deception is one way to describe it but don't you mean murder?"

"Justina was the one who killed Markell?" T-Roc was shocked. Although he knew Markell was dead, he never thought Justina was the one who murdered him.

"Yes, I thought you knew." Desmond regretted being the one to share the information.

"I learned they had been romantically involved and she also was partaking in his illegal activities but murder...damn!" T-Roc folded his hands on the back of his head and looked up at the ceiling. "I've been so focused on my own bullshit, I missed how far gone my daughter had become. Some fuckin' father I am."

"Don't be so hard on yourself. Yes, Justina has a lot of childhood issues she's dealing with but she was a grown woman, when she made her choices. And she's taking responsibility for her actions." Desmond came from behind his desk and stood directly in front of T-Roc. "Not sure if she's mentioned it, but Justina has been seeing a therapist and a psychiatrist. It was part of our agreement before moving forward with our relationship. She was making significant progress but of course, the kidnapping of our son, has been a major setback."

"Then we have to get him back because I'm not losing my daughter. I've failed her many times in the past but never again," T-Roc promised.

Chapter Six

Survival

Angel was still incensed, when she grabbed her purse and keys, leaving the office. "Elsa, I'll be out of the office for the rest of the day. I'm on my way to take care of some important business, so don't disturb me."

"There shouldn't be much of a reason to disturb you, since we basically have no girls working," Elsa mumbled under her breath.

"Why don't you speak up. Clearly you have a lot to say." Angel stopped mid step, waiting for Elsa's response.

"No disrespect, Angel. I completely understand why you're pissed off. But punishing every single girl, even the ones that did show up for work, is a bit extreme. Not to mention, it's hurting the business financially and our clients too."

"Didn't you get your paycheck yesterday... then let me worry about the finances." She snapped at Elsa. "In regards to those duplicitous dummies, they need to know how it feels to not work here for a week. If you reward people who are disloyal to you, then best believe they'll do it again."

"But what about the handful of girls that weren't disloyal. Don't they deserve to work?"

"That's where you're wrong. They were disloyal too. The moment they knew what was going down and didn't bring it to our attention, they fucked up. We had to practically twist Pricilla's arm for her to come clean. If they do some dumb shit like this again, I'm done. Because at this very moment, I'm sick of them bitches. I'ma hire some help and get rid of them bitches," Angel raged.

"I apologize for getting you more upset," Elsa said, realizing it was wise of her to shut up. It wasn't the right time, to defend the women who betrayed her boss.

"I have to go." Angel threw up her hand and left the building. Once in her car, she headed to Brickell Ave in downtown Miami. When she entered the minimalist, contemporary, open floor office space, a thin red head receptionist greeted her.

"How may I help you?"

"I'm here to see your boss."

"Excuse me?"

"You know, the one who keeps you employed." Angel specified, already past being impatient.

"That would be me," an unassuming woman said, coming out from one of the offices.

"You're not who I'm looking for either. I want to see your boss, Juan Martinez." The two women eyed each other and Angel was ready to lay both of them down, if they didn't stop stalling.

"Meredith, I'll take care of this," the unassuming woman told the receptionist. "Miss, I'm Valerie," she said, extending her hand but Angel left it right there in the air.

"Unless, you're going to take me to your boss, I don't care who you are."

"I see." The woman cleared her throat. "Can I tell Mr. Martinez who is here to see him."

"Angel Blaze. He'll recognize the name, as I'm sure you do too."

"Yes. Please follow me."

Angel followed behind Valerie. Her hand firmly clutching the gun in her purse. Angel doubted she'd need to use it but was prepared just in case. When Valerie opened the door, the man seemed startled she walked in without knocking. His look of surprise, then shifted to anger, until he noticed Angel standing behind her.

"Mr. Martinez, An..."

"I know who she is," he said cutting Valerie off. "Mrs. Blaze, please come sit down," he said, graciously.

"No need to sit because I won't be staying long." Angel got straight to the point. "It's come to my attention, you've been trying to get my girl's to come work for you. Offering them all sorts of incentives. Unfortunately, many of them took the bait but that ends today. Businesswoman to businessman, Angel's Girls are off limit. It took some time but I've built a very successful business and have a solid reputation. You need to respect that and move on. There are plenty of other women in Miami, go hire them."

"But I heard you have the best," Juan smiled.

"I do because I spent a lot of time and money grooming them. I suggest you hold a casting call and find you some chicks to groom too but I like I stated, mine are off limits," Angel reiterated.

"I'm sorry, I can't do that. Those women have the option of working for anyone they want. It's called freedom of choice. Finding escorts for well to do men is big business and like with everything I do, I want to be successful. Which means I want the best girls and you have them, Angel."

"You don't want to make an enemy of me but if you keep fuckin' around in my territory, then that's what you'll be."

"Beautiful and ballsy," Juan smirked. "I would ask you to be my wife but I know you're already married. Your husband is quite the boxer. I hope you won't bring him here to rough me up."

"Save your sarcasm. I'm more than capable of handling you without my husband."

"I don't doubt that for a moment." Juan stroked his hand through his thick black curls and bit down on his lip. Angel sensed he was upset and gripped her gun even tighter, not sure what the hot blooded Latina would do next.

"I hate feeling disrespected." Juan finally spoke and said.

"Then I guess we have one thing in common because I do too. And you have me feeling extremely disrespected, Mr. Martinez."

"I tell you what." Juan eased up on his tense mood. "I'll think about what you said and will be in touch. I know how to find you."

"You do that. But don't take too long, or I might start feeling disrespected again." Angel let her words linger for a moment, allowing Juan to take it in. It was a subtle threat and by the stiffness in Juan's jaw, she knew he caught it. Now Angel had to make sure she could back it up.

Aaliyah was up bright and early to start her day with baby Desi, who she decided to rename Elijah. She went into his room and he was still sleeping peacefully. She couldn't get over, how he was such a good baby. He only cried when he was hungry or wet. Like anything or anyone you invest a lot of your time in and take care of,

Aaliyah had developed deep feelings for the little tot.

"You are too perfect for words," Aaliyah gushed. Elijah had a head full of hair and she couldn't resist gently rubbing her fingers through it. "I've completely fallen in love with a child that isn't mine," she admitted out loud for the very first time. Since Elijah was still asleep, Aaliyah decided to take her shower and get dressed before Lorita arrived.

"Fuck! I thought Lorita wasn't supposed to be here for another twenty minutes," Aaliyah huffed, turning off the water. She wrapped a towel around her body, before going to open the door.

"Good morning! I brought over your favorite muffins from that bakery you love," Precious grinned widely, holding up two bags.

"Mother, what are you doing here so early?"

"I told you. I wanted to surprise you with your favorite muffins."

"You came all the way to the city, to bring me muffins?!"

"It isn't the only reason," Precious disclosed. "I also wanted to see your new place. I haven't been over since you first moved in."

"I'm still getting it together. It's not worth showing just yet."

"That's totally fine. I'm sure you've done some decorating," Precious said, stepping forward to go inside but Aaliyah was trying to block her passage. "If I didn't know better, I would say you're trying to keep me from coming inside."

"Don't be silly," Aaliyah laughed, stepping aside. Her heart was racing, praying Elijah didn't wake up and start crying. She was trying to come up with some sort of lie she could tell her mother just in case but she knew Precious was way too smart to believe any of it.

"It looks beautiful in here. You've added a gorgeous light fixture," Precious enthused, admiring the crystal drop round chandelier, draped with hundreds of glass droplets in alternating teardrop and raindrop shapes. "I love the curtains too. And who gave you these stunning flowers? Let me guess…Supreme. He always picks out the best flower arrangements."

"They are exquisite but actually Angel is the sender. I was pleasantly surprised when they were delivered yesterday. It was a sweet gesture. She wanted me to know, she's thinking of me," Aaliyah smiled, taking a whiff of the floral scent.

"That was sweet of Angel. I'm really happy you all have become close. Having a sister who loves you, is a beautiful thing."

"I agree."

"Now let's go upstairs. I'm sure you've done some amazing things to your bedroom."

"Maybe another time," Aaliyah smiled, keeping her cool. "Mother, It's great you stopped by but I was just about to get in the shower. I'm really running late for class."

"Well, I'm sure you can at least sit down and have a muffin with me," Precious said, putting down her belongings, ready to get comfortable.

"That must be my classmate from school!" Aaliyah was breathing a sigh of relief, when she heard the doorbell. "Lorita, hi! I'm so sorry I'm not dressed yet. I know we're running late for class but my mother stopped by unexpectedly," she explained, prepping her nanny and partner in crime before letting her inside.

"Try to hurry. You know how our teacher hates when anyone is late," Lorita said, playing along.

"Hi Lorita, I'm Precious. It's nice to meet you."

Aaliyah could tell her mother was sizing

up her so called classmate. Luckily, Lorita was around the same age as Aaliyah, which made it seem very plausible, they would've connected at school.

"Nice to meet you too," Lorita replied. Fortunately she was used to playing roles, so she didn't flinch at Precious scrutinizing her on the low.

"I promise, we'll share muffins another time but I really need to get ready," Aaliyah said, gathering up her mother's things, nearly throwing her out the door.

"Okay, well it was good seeing you if only briefly," Precious said, kissing Aaliyah on the cheek.

"It was good seeing you too...I love you." Aaliyah led her mother by the arm to the door, making sure she didn't make any stops on her way out.

"That was close." Lorita looked over at Aaliyah, who was leaning against the door.

"Too close. I can't wait to leave New York for good. I'm sure this pop up visit from my mother is just the first of many," Aaliyah panted. "I can't afford to take these type of chances."

"You're right. If anyone sees you with a baby,

they'll quickly put two and two together. Then we'll both be in jail on kidnapping charges."

"Lorita, I got this covered. Elijah and I will be leaving soon and you'll be free to run off and spend all that money I've given you."

"I can't spend the money if I'm locked up," Lorita shot back.

"Nobody is going to jail. I planned out everything perfectly. Just follow my lead and all will be fine. Now if you excuse me, I need to check on Elijah."

Aaliyah headed upstairs and for the first time, a sense of nervousness came over her. So far, her plan had zero hiccups but she never considered her mother becoming a problem. Once Aaliyah moved out of her parent's house in New Jersey and got her own place in the city, she figured she didn't have to worry about them discovering what she'd been up to. But keeping her distance from her mother was only making Precious more nosey.

We might need to leave New York sooner than I expected, Aaliyah thought to herself, as she held baby Elijah close to her heart.

Chapter Seven

One More Chance

"Desmond, thank you for seeing me. I truly appreciate it," Angel asserted, when she walked into his office.

"If I said I was happy to see you, it would be a lie. But you were persistent and didn't leave me much of a choice. So, what can I do for you, Angel?"

"I know you weren't pleased how we ended things but…"

"But nothing," Desmond scoffed, cutting Angel off. "You demanded I fire my wife. Instead of putting her through any unnecessary stress, I sold you my share of Angel's Girls for basically peanuts. So, I don't know what else you could want from me."

"Under the circumstances, it was best Justina not be there. We already had issues and once I found out she was the one, responsible for Dale finding out what Aaliyah's father had done, there was no way I could work with her."

"You mean after you illegally recorded Justina's personal conversations, with me as a matter of fact. Regardless, you made this same argument months ago and I gave you what you wanted. So again, why are you here?"

"You're right. It was a mistake for me to come," Angel said, turning around to leave and Desmond had no intentions of stopping her, so she stopped herself.

At this point, Desmond had put his head down and was back to work. He was thrilled his impromptu meeting with Angel only took a few minutes and she was on her way out the door.

"Desmond, I need your help."

"Excuse me?" he glanced up, taken aback by

what he heard. "I know you didn't ask me for my help."

"Yes I did and you know I must need it, if I'm coming to you," Aaliyah swallowed her pride and said.

"I'm tempted to tell you, to get the hell out my office," Desmond said, tossing his pen down and leaning back in his chair." But I'm a tad bit curious, as to what you're about to say next."

"Do you know a man named Juan Martinez?"

"No, I can't say that I do. Why?"

"Because he's trying to put me out of business. He's been going after all of my girls and most of them have taken the bait, working other gigs behind my back. I went to see him and I don't believe he has any intentions of leaving my company alone."

"It's not like you need the money, why don't you let him have Angel's Girls and save yourself the headache."

"Because that company is mine. I started it and I'm not about to let some fast talking, wannabe pimp take what I built," Angel yelled.

"You say you want my help. What can I do?"

"I want us to become partners again."

"You can't be serious," Desmond grunted.

"I'll be the first to admit, when we were partners, business was excellent. You brought in new clientele and you had a great rapport with all the women working for us. I never had any issue with you, it was your wife. But now that Justina is home taking care of a newborn baby, I'm sure she has no interest in coming to work."

"I guess you haven't heard."

"Heard what?"

"Our son was kidnapped and he's still missing."

"Omigoodness! Desmond, I had no idea. I'm so sorry!" Angel exclaimed, putting her hand over her mouth. "Darien and I went away on vacation and we just got back recently, so I've been completely out the loop. Do the police have any leads?"

"Unfortunately no."

"I know an excellent private investigator. He was the one who helped me find my father. Maybe he can help you find your son."

"I have my own people on it but I appreciate the offer."

"If you change your mind let me know," Angel said, sitting down next to Desmond. "I know

Justina must be going crazy. How is she holding up?"

"You don't have to pretend you care how my wife is doing."

"We both know I'm not a fan of Justina but I wouldn't wish this on my worst enemy. No woman should have their child kidnapped. This has to be hard on you too."

"It is but I'm dealing."

"Is the kidnapper asking for some sort of ransom? You're a successful and high profile businessman here in Miami and Justina has a very famous father. I'm assuming this is a money shakedown."

"If it is, whoever is responsible hasn't made any money demands. Justina believes the nanny she hired is in on it."

"Really...did you tell the police?"

"Yes but the nanny has vanished. Her name, address...none of it's legit. It's a nightmare."

"We will find your son," Angel stated, putting her hand on Desmond's arm. "I promise you. You're not in this alone."

"I'm guessing all this kindness, is your way of guilting me into helping you."

"No. Honestly, if I had known about your

son, I would've never come to you and asked. The last thing you need is the stress that comes from work."

"Work is exactly what I need," Desmond nodded. "Coming here has kept me from completely losing it. A partnership with you again, will be another outlet to keep me from going insane."

"Listen, I'm not gonna try to change your mind because I do need you but only if you're sure."

"I'm positive. Partners." Desmond held out his hand."

"Partners." Angel smiled, shaking Desmond's hand.

"Since Supreme likes to tell you everything, I'm sure you're aware we have a lot going on right now," Nico mocked, when Precious showed up to his house unannounced. "So whatever you have going on, will have to wait."

"Save the sarcasm. I'm here about Aaliyah. I'm sure our daughter supersedes any business you're dealing with."

"I don't like Supreme but I know he loves

Aaliyah. If something was wrong with her, he would drop everything. But he's with Lorenzo and Genesis right now, trying to figure out, how to get us out of this bullshit we're in. I also know, you would go to him before coming to me. So, I'm assuming you already brought your theatrics to Supreme and he dismissed them, now you're coming to me," Nico summarized.

"You think you know me so well."

"It's not a think, it's a fact," Nico stated, getting his stuff together to leave. "I'm on my way to join them, so like I said, whatever you want to talk about, has to wait."

"Nico, it can't wait!" Precious shouted, grabbing his keys off the counter, as he was reaching for them, so he couldn't leave." Our daughter is in real trouble. Do you know she's planning some around the world tour? It's bullshit. Aaliyah has a hissy fit when a flight is longer than four hours! All I'm asking is for you to speak with her," Precious pleaded.

"So you know, I speak to Aaliyah daily," Nico responded with irritation. "You're reaching. Despite what you might think, Aaliyah is in a good place. I think leaving town will do her some good. Miami and even being here in New York, is only a reminder of everything she's loss. People heal differently, Precious. Everyone isn't like you."

"What the fuck is that supposed to mean, Nico?"

"It means, give Aaliyah space to grieve. If she needs to go away and travel, take some classes, or work on a new project, let her. Stop stalking our daughter and allow the girl to breathe."

"Is that what Aaliyah said I'm doing...stalking her?" Precious was visibly offended by what Nico said.

"I can't do this wit' you right now. We got serious problems that have to be handled asap, before dead bodies start accumulating. We not only dealing wit' that crazy fuck Arnez but this new nigga Maverick, is now in the mix. Aaliyah is fine. Go find something else to worry about, Precious. Now let's go. I have to meet Genesis," Nico said, snatching his keys out of Precious's hand, before she got slick and decided to toss them somewhere. Leaving him stuck, to listen to what he considered to be baseless conspiracy theories about his daughter.

Nico's dismissive tone only fueled Precious's determination to figure out what was going on with Aaliyah. The more everyone tried to make her feel she was being delusional or paranoid, it had the exact opposite effect. A mother knows her child and if no one was willing to help, then Precious decided she would get it done herself.

Chapter Eight

Whatever It Takes

"Clarissa, thank you for taking me to get my nails done and for this pedicure. I've been so broke, I haven't been able to pamper myself in what feels like forever." Dominique had her eyes closed, enjoying the foot massage she was getting from the nail tech.

"Girl, anytime. Trust me, I know what it feels like to be short on cash. I'm just glad your body is healing from the car accident and you're starting to feel like yourself again."

"No doubt, it's been a long time coming," Dominique exhaled, welcoming some relaxation. "I really believed I was gonna die that night. Taren was a fuckin' looney tune. I'm so damn happy, she'll never be able to hurt anybody else again."

"Yeah, she may be dead but she's left her mark. She killed my best friend and don't forget all those people that either died or were injured when she set off that bomb in the club. Yo, she was a sick fuck foreal," Clarissa said, remembering all the dead bodies Taren left behind.

"I still get teary eyed thinking about Mrs. Armstrong," Dominque said somberly. "I wanna put the entire Taren nightmare behind me and get my life back. That starts with me getting a job. SInce I've completed my physical therapy and the doctor has cleared me to dance again, I'm hoping I can start making some money to pay my own way."

"With things being so tight, I'm sure Angel wouldn't mind loaning you some money to help you out. She's a rich bitch," Clarissa winked.

"Angel has already done so much for me. Besides the money she gave me for my bills, I told you she's the one who paid all my medical expenses. I wouldn't feel right asking her for anything else."

"I feel you. What about Desmond? As far as I'm concerned that nigga owe you," Clarissa smacked her lips. "You were a real money earner at the club. The customers loved you. It's not your fault his wife found out ya had sex."

"Yeah, it's my fault for spilling the tea. I couldn't help myself though. That woman drives me crazy and it's not just because I wanted her man," Dominique laughed.

"From what you told me, she's a piece of work but I know she's hurting right about now, Desmond too."

"Hurting...why? Did something happen?"

"You didn't hear about their baby being kidnapped? Desmond's been trying to keep it lowkey but I heard it's been on the news a few times. I could've sworn I said something to you about it. But maybe I didn't because honestly, I only found out about it the other day. I overheard his assistant on the phone discussing it."

"What! That's crazy! I don't even watch the news, so of course I wouldn't have heard about it on there. And since I haven't been working at the club, I count on you to tell me all the gossip. That's horrible!"

"Yep but he still be coming to work. Probably to keep his mind off what's going on in his personal life. He always seemed so cold blooded to me but your child being kidnapped, would make anyone crack."

"Poor Desmond. He must really be going through it right now." Dominique stared off sadly.

Clarissa cut her eyes at her friend. "After firing you from your job and cutting you completely off to appease his wife, you still got it bad for that man." Clarissa shook her head. "Let it go, Dominique. Desmond ain't the nigga for you."

Dominique heard what Clarissa was saying but she wasn't listening. Instead, she was daydreaming about the one night of passion she shared with Desmond. Something she found herself doing on a regular basis. Dominque wanted to free herself of this hold Desmond had over her but the heart wants what the heart wants.

"Elsa, get Aaliyah on the phone for me. For some reason I'm getting really poor reception on my cell," Angel said, headed to her office.

"Sure thing."

"Excuse me! Angel, can I speak to you for a second." Shayla ran up, catching Angel by surprise.

"What is it?"

"I'm Shayla...I work for Angel's Girls."

"I know who you are and if I recall, you were let go when Justina stopped working here."

"That's the thing, I was hoping to get my job back," Shayla said, putting her hand on her hip. "I mean, I felt I brought a lot to the company. My clients were really feelin' me a lot. You know what I'm sayin'."

Before Angel could reply, Elsa interrupted their exchange. "Are you sure I have the right number for Aaliyah?"

"Yeah why?"

"Because at first I heard someone answer, then a baby crying in the background and the phone went dead. It was really strange."

"Maybe you dialed the wrong number. Try again," Angel snapped. "Oh wait, come to think of it, it was probably Lorita's baby you heard."

"Lorita...who's that?" Elsa asked, not familiar with the name.

"A friend of hers. One time when I was on the phone with Aaliyah, I heard a baby. She told me it was her friend Lorita's little boy," Angel casually explained to Elsa. "She spends a lot of time at Aaliyah's place."

"Got you. So, should I call back?" Elsa questioned.

"Just forget it. I'll call her myself when I get to my office," she said brushing Elsa off, wanting to finish her conversation with Shayla. "Listen, I'm extremely busy. I understand you want your job back but the bottom line is, I don't think you're a good fit for Angel's Girls."

"Why, cause I ain't all uppity and prissy," Shayla snarled.

"More like, you're a little bit too rough around the edges for my taste. But good luck on your future endeavors. Now excuse me, I have work to do. Elsa, can I see you in my office for a minute," Angel said, leaving Shayla reeling.

"What a self-righteous piece of shit!" Shayla fumed, leaning on Elsa's desk. *How dare she treat me like I'm beneath her. Now I understand why Taren couldn't stand her stuck-up ass and my cousin is dead because of princess Angel,* Shayla thought to herself. Shayla continued her rant until something on Elsa's desk caught her eye. "Lookie here!" Her eyes lit up. She grabbed the large envelope off Elsa's desk, exiting the building.

Precious stood quietly, replaying what Supreme said, wishing she heard him wrong. "I had no idea Justina already had her baby and now he's missing. That's unbelievable."

"It is. As much as we need T-Roc here with us to deal with Arnez and help find out what happened to Genesis, I understand him going to Miami to be with his daughter. I do hope the police find his grandson."

"Yes. Does he have any idea who took him?"

"No, none at all. Baby, I would love to stay here and talk to you some more but I have to get to the city," Supreme said, kissing Precious. "Call me if you need anything."

"Okay, I will. I love you."

"Love you too."

Precious felt herself becoming ill. All her worrying hadn't been in vain. T-Roc might've not had a clue who kidnapped his grandson but

Precious was damn near positive she knew who did. But before confirming her worst fears, she wanted to speak to someone first.

When Precious pulled up to the brownstone on Park Avenue, she took a deep breath and mentally prepared herself for the finessing she was about to do. She touched up her lipstick, fluffed her hair before exiting out her car.

"Precious, what are you doing here?" Chantal questioned, when she opened her front door, with a bewildered glare on her face.

"I came over to see how you're doing." Chantal continued to give Precious the same baffled stare. "Supreme told me what happened to Justina. I'm so sorry."

"Oh please, you can't stand my daughter and you hate me even more," Chantal sniped, ready to slam the door in Precious's face.

"Wait!" Precious put her hand up to keep the door from shutting.

"I'm not going to stand here and listen to you gloat over my family's misfortune."

"Chantal, I would never do that. When I

heard about what happened to Justina, it hit a nerve. Our daughters grew up together. We've had our differences but we're both mothers and I understand your pain."

"Come in," Chantal said, still weary of Precious's sudden kind gesture.

"Thank you."

"Can I get you something to drink?" Chantal offered.

"A glass of wine but only if you'll join me."

"Two glasses of wine coming right up," Chantal beamed, always looking for an excuse to have a drink.

After an hour or so of small talk and Precious stroking Chantal's ego, she felt it's was time to circle back to the real reason she showed up at the door, of a woman she couldn't stand.

"Supreme mentioned T-Roc was in Miami to see Justina. I'm surprised you didn't go with him."

"My husband can be so controlling." Chantal rolled her eyes, sipping on her third or fourth glass of wine. Precious had lost count, as she was still babysitting her first one. "Of course I wanted to go be with my daughter but T-Roc insisted I stay here."

"Why is that?"

"He tends to think I can be over dramatic. Probably the same way Supreme sees you," Chantal giggled. "T-Roc said with Justina already being so traumatized, me being there would just make things worse. He said I can join him in a couple of days, after he's done playing hero," Chantal said sarcastically.

"Poor Justina. No mother deserves this. Do you know exactly when you're grandson was kidnapped?"

"Of course! I'll never forget when my daughter called me in the middle of the night, completely frantic. It was July 11th. She was beside herself. Thank goodness, T-Roc was home that night and not out with one of his mistresses. He was able to calm her down. He's a terrible husband but a great father. I have to admit, our son and daughter adore him," Chantal shrugged.

"Do the police have any leads?"

"No! Although the nanny has suspiciously gone missing. No one has seen or heard from her since my sweet grandson disappeared." Chantal's eyes watered up. "Whoever did this, will have hell to pay. They'll either end up dead or rot in prison for the rest of their life."

"Hopefully they'll catch him soon," Precious

said.

"You think it's a man too? So do I!" Chantal exclaimed. "I told T-Roc that only a man could do something so bold and cruel. That nanny is probably working for him. Once they track her down. I'm positive they'll find the real culprit."

"I agree."

"I wasn't going to mention it but since we're bonding as mothers, I'm sorry for what happened to your daughter. Losing her husband and child… my gosh I don't think I could survive it. How is Aaliyah?"

"She's getting better. Aaliyah's been staying with us, at our estate in New Jersey. She's barely left the house since I brought her back from Miami," Precious said, establishing an alibi for her daughter, just in case one was ever needed.

"That's wonderful. Right now she needs her family more than ever."

"Yes, family is so important, Chantal. That's why, although our daughters are going through such a difficult time, we have to remain united. We've had our differences and unfortunately Aaliyah and Justina aren't on speaking terms right now but we have to set a good example for them. Show them the importance of sticking together."

"Never in a million years, did I think I'd hear those words coming out your mouth. I mean neither of us are saints, we're both much better sinners," Chantal winked. "I think that's why we've never gotten along. We're too much alike. But I'll admit, I'm enjoying this female bonding and I genuinely appreciate your concern for Justina."

"To new beginnings and new friendships." Precious raised her glass and finished off the remainder of her wine. "I would love to stay, as I could chat with you all day but wife and mother duties call. Please keep me abreast of what's happening with Justina and your sweet grandbaby. I'm always here if you need someone to talk to." Precious gave Chantal a warm hug.

Precious went from sitting on a couch in Chantal's living room, to getting on her cell phone, the moment her heels touched the cement of the upper east side street.

"Hi Carlos, it's me Precious Mills."

"Good afternoon, Mrs. Mills, how are you?"

"I'm good and you?"

"Feeling great! Are you calling to let us know you'll be using the jet?"

"No, I was hoping you could help me with

something else."

"I'll do my best, what do you need?"

"You know my daughter Aaliyah."

"Of course I know Miss Aaliyah."

Do you know the last time she used the private jet?"

"Let me check the books. Just a moment," Carlos said putting Precious on a brief hold. "Nothing this year, Mrs. Mills. I'm not showing anything since Christmas."

"Really." Precious briefly felt a sigh of relief but she had to be sure. "Can you check and see if anyone used the jet on July 11th."

"Sure. Yes someone did use the jet."

"Who?"

"That's strange, a name wasn't written down. It just says female passenger with child."

"Thanks, Carlos. I appreciate your assistance."

"Of course, Mrs. Mills. Anytime. Make sure you tell your husband I said hello."

"Will do." Precious hung up with Carlos and wasted no time calling her daughter. Not surprisingly, Aaliyah didn't answer her phone. "Aaliyah, this is your mother but you already know that! You better call me the moment you get this message. I'm on my way over right now. We need to talk!"

Precious had pulled her fair share of stunts but kidnapping another woman's child, was even too much for her to fully grasp. She didn't want to believe her daughter had gone completely over the edge but there weren't that many coincidences in the world. It was all making sense now. Aaliyah moving out, her odd behavior and the way she rushed her out of her townhouse.

"Oh gosh! Aaliyah has the baby there with her!" Precious screamed, speeding off to her daughter's place.

Chapter Nine

Opening Pandora's Box

"Girl, how you doin'!" Shayla was extra animated when Justina opened the door. "Give me a hug. I ain't seen you in a minute."

"I thought that was you I saw on the security camera," Justina said, completely unenthusiastic as Shayla hugged her tightly. "What are you doing here and how did you find out where I live?"

"I tried calling you but you changed your

number. Here, I brought you something," Shayla announced, handing Justina the large envelope she swiped off Elsa's desk. "Your address is on there."

"What is this?" Justina held up the envelope.

"I think it was a bunch of a mail that had piled up and Elsa planned on sending to you. I thought I would personally deliver it," Shayla winked, barging her way into Justina's house. "Damn, this a nice ass crib."

"Thanks," Justina rubbed her eyes, closing the door. "Shayla, I'm really exhausted. I appreciate you bringing this over but I was just about to go to bed."

"In the middle of the day...oh wow, look at that pool out there," Shayla babbled, totally ignoring what Justina said. "Damn, I shoulda brought my bikini." She opened the French doors leading outside, to what was designed to look like a roman bath of the ancient times, with marble and intricate mosaic tiles. There was even a floating pavilion placed within the pool itself. "Chile, this the type of crib I need to be living in."

"I promise to invite you over another day but right now..."

"Justina, girl I'm sorry. Look at me gettin'

sidetracked," Shayla closed the French doors and came back inside the house. "Listen, the real reason I stopped by is because I need a job. Angel tossed me to the side after you stop working there. I was in her office, begging her to put me back on and she dismissed me like I was some trash."

"I'm sorry to hear that but..."

"The nerve of that heifa!" Shayla continued rambling on, only allowing Justina to get a few words in. "While I was groveling, Angel kept payin' me dust. Then that naggin' ass Elsa, was whining like always," she smacked, twisting her neck. "Talkin' 'bout Angel gave her the wrong number, cause when she called Aaliyah, she heard a baby in the background. I'm like who fuckin' cares. Don't you see me tryna go back to work and get these coins. Them hoes so stupid. That's why I need you Justina. You 'bout that money and I know you'll hook a sista up."

"Back up a minute," Justina said, quickly coming out of her sleepy stupor, after what Shayla mentioned. "Did you say you heard a baby?"

"I ain't hear shit. Oh fuck! You done had yo' baby. My bad! I forgot you was even pregnant. You done lost all yo' baby weight. Maybe too much," Shayla commented, only now noticing, Justina's somewhat frail figure. "That explains why you ain't lookin' too hot," she nodded. "You know normally, you 'bout the baddest thing walkin'. I ain't wanna say nothin' but I was nervous for you. But the baby thing explains it," she rambled on. "You must be up all night. Did you have a girl or a boy?"

"A boy but we can talk about that later. Tell me exactly what you heard."

"Oh, so I was begging Angel's ass for my..."

"Not that part. What Elsa said." Justina wanted to scream at Shayla to shut the fuck up with all the extra shit but her pills had her feeling lethargic, so she opted for a more mellow approach.

"Elsa didn't really say shit. She was being worrisome per usual," Shayla shrugged.

"I get that part but what did you hear her say, when you were talking to Angel?"

"Elsa asked Angel was she sure she gave her the right number because when she called Aaliyah, someone answered, she heard a baby crying and then the person hung up. Angel told her dizzy ass don't worry about it. She know Elsa dumb as dirt too. She probably did dial the wrong number. No wait, my bad."

"Your bad what?"

"That's what Angel said at first. Then she remembered Aaliyah had a friend named, Laponzo, Laquita...something like that, who had a baby boy. Just like you, girl!" Shayla giggled, like the shit was funny.

"What about Aaliyah's friend?"

"Angel explained to dumb, dumb, the girl has a baby boy and she be at Aaliyah's crib a lot and that's probably the baby she heard crying in the back. So, Elsa wasn't being her normally silly self. She didn't dial the wrong number. Now, can we get back to me and my job situation. I'm sick of talkin' about Elsa idiotic ass. Are you gonna help a sista out or what? Cause Angel ain't shit!"

"That fuckin' bitch!" Justina blurted loudly.

"Ain't Angel a bitch and I don't mean the good kinda bitch neither, like you, Justina. And she such a fuckin' snob too," Shayla made sure to add.

Shayla was under the impression they shared a mutual disgust for Angel, having no clue her little commentary opened Pandora's Box and would send Justina full throttle. Through all her despair, Aaliyah had never been on her radar. She figured the fraudulent nanny she hired was somehow involved in the kidnapping but never her former best friend. She was aware Aaliyah had a miscarriage, so there wasn't a doubt in her mind, the baby Elsa heard crying in the background was her son Desi. Justina had gotten so used to being doped up on pills, she'd forgotten how angry she could get. Flashes of ripping Aaliyah's head off, consumed her mind.

"Justina, are okay?" Shayla asked, seeing how enraged she appeared to be."I mean I know you can't stand Angel neither but fuck her! She ain't worth the energy. Let's get back to me! I got bills to pay. Hell, I wanna get on yo' level but baby steps."

"Have a seat, Shayla." Justina's demeanor went from being sluggish to razor sharp focused. "If you do what I say, all of your financial troubles will disappear like magic."

"Now we talkin'! I'm listening, girl. Speak to me!" Shayla's ears were wide open, as she hung on to every word Justina spoke. She always yearned to be besties with a woman on Justina's level but felt it was way out of her reach. If being a ride or die for her would make them closer, then Shayla was all in.

Precious pounded so hard on the door, it sounded like she was about to break it down. "Open the door, Aaliyah!" She shouted over and over again.

"Aaliyah isn't here." Lorita flung open the door and said to an agitated Precious.

"Move out my way!" Precious demanded. Lorita had enough sense not to protest, seeing the fire in her eyes.

"I'm not sure when Aaliyah will be back. Can I help you with something?"

"Save the polite jibber jabber and tell me where my daughter is."

"I'm not sure. I think she had a class."

"Save the lies! I know my daughter isn't taking any fuckin' classes, unless it's parenting courses," Precious mocked. "Where is the baby?"

"Baby? I don't know what you're talking about. Aaliyah doesn't have a baby," Lorita answered innocently.

"You're good. You sound very sincere. If I didn't know better, I would even believe you. Tell me Lorita, how did you meet my daughter?"

"At school. Like Aaliyah told you, we're taking classes together."

Precious flung her arm with such quickness, Lorita didn't realize what happened, until she was pinned up against the wall. "I'm not the woman to lie to. I will break your neck," Precious warned. "I'm going to ask you one last time. Where is my daughter?"

"Mother! What are you doing?!" Aaliyah came in the house and yelled. "Let her go!"

"Fine. She's no use to me now." Precious released Lorita from her grasp, walking over to Aaliyah. "You have a lot of explaining to do, young lady."

"Mother, what is your problem? You come over to my house, physically assaulting my friend."

"Oh, I thought she was just your classmate. I had no idea the two of you were friends." Precious glanced over at Lorita. "Would this be the same friend, who brought Justina's baby to New York on our private jet?"

"Justina's baby...I had no idea she even gave birth," Aaliyah shrugged, closing the front door.

"Really? So, who was the woman with the baby, you let use our jet?"

"That must be a mistake."

"The mistake was you taking Justina's child. And I hope whatever Aaliyah promised you, is worth all the years you're about to spend in prison," Precious said, now directing her words towards Lorita. "When you crossed state lines, your kidnapping became a federal crime. Are you willing to do that bid?"

"Lorita, don't listen to my mother. She's good at using scare tactics. We've done nothing wrong,"

"Nothing wrong. You kidnapped another woman's child! Clearly, you've gone insane."

"Mother, I'm not crazy!"

"Then you better start pretending like you are because it's the only defense that might keep you from doing twenty years in prison," Precious spit.

"I don't know where all this is coming from but I don't have Justina's baby. Feel free to look through this entire place, there's no baby here," Aaliyah stated matter of factly.

Precious didn't hesitate to take Aaliyah up on her offer. "You stay right here. I'll be back."

"How in the hell did your mother find out it was me on the plane?" Lorita said under her breath, when Precious was no longer within view.

"I don't know but it doesn't matter. We made sure this place is devoid of all things baby related. My mother won't find anything. It's one thing to think something, it's another to have proof, so keep your cool," Aaliyah advised.

"Here she comes," Lorita whispered when she saw Precious coming down the stairs.

"Did you find what you were looking for, Mother?" Aaliyah questioned in a smug tone.

"It doesn't matter. I know you have Justina's baby, Aaliyah. Luckily for you, nobody suspects you're responsible for the kidnapping, which means we still have time to fix this mess. But the longer her son is missing, the more problematic this becomes. Justina will do everything possible to make sure you're punished."

"I didn't kidnap her baby but I'm not worried about Justina being a problem. She's no match for me," Aaliyah smirked.

"But her father is. If T-Roc finds out you kidnapped his grandson, it's going to take more than Supreme and Nico to save you. Do you understand what I'm telling you?" Precious raised her eyebrow, wondering if she was reaching her daughter. "Do you remember the favors T-Roc called in, to get his batshit crazy wife off, for killing Sway? Don't underestimate him. T-Roc's out of your league, little girl."

"Everything you're saying is irrelevant because like I told you, I don't have Justina's baby. This is the first I'm even hearing about her son being kidnapped. I don't like Justina but it's very unfortunate what happened to her. Maybe I'll send her a care package."

"Have it your way. But I can promise you, when I tell both your fathers what you've done, be prepared for the consequences," Precious warned before leaving.

"Stop her!" Lorita implored. "We don't need her telling anyone else."

"When my mother popped up unexpectedly a few weeks ago, I knew she might be a problem. That's why we temporarily moved Elijah to your mother's house."

"Yeah but it's no longer a might, she is a problem!" Lorita screamed.

"True but now I'll have to settle on Plan B."

"Which is?"

"I was waiting for Elijah's new birth certificate and the other paperwork to get done before taking him out of the country. Instead of waiting here in New York, we'll fly somewhere else until everything is ready and where my mother can't locate me. Once I get it, we'll disappear."

"And what about me?" Lorita asked.

"I suggest you take all that money I gave you and get out of town. Go someplace far away and start over. I recommend you leave tonight."

"Tonight! Oh my gosh. This can't be happening," Lorita said, becoming frantic. "You're not worried about your mother turning you in?"

"To the police…please!" Aaliyah scoffed. "No matter how furious my mother might be at me, she's loyal to a fault. But the threat of her telling Nico and Supreme is enough to get me the hell outta town, asap. You on the other hand, won't be safe from their wrath, so I strongly advise you to leave."

"Where are you going?" Lorita questioned when Aaliyah ran upstairs.

"I'll be right back." Aaliyah hurried off before soon returning with a duffel bag. "Here's a little extra dough for being inconvenienced," she said, handing the bag to her partner in crime. "But take my advice, Lorita and leave NYC immediately."

"So this is it. After tonight I'll never see you

or Elijah again?"

"You knew eventually we would part ways. That was always the plan from the beginning."

"I know but I assumed you would change your mind and ask me to come with you. Do you really wanna be in some foreign country alone with a baby?"

"You have a point but I figured you wouldn't want to leave your family."

"I didn't and I still don't but now that your family knows what you did and I have to leave town anyway, why not come with you and Elijah. I really do love that little boy," Lorita smiled.

"You are great with him and having the additional support would be wonderful," Aaliyah acknowledged. But I think it's better for us to travel separately. Once I decide where we're going next, I'll send for you. But Lorita, I need you to keep a very low profile. My family is extremely resourceful, so don't stay at your mother's house. They'll track you down. Are we clear."

"Yes. I have a friend I can stay with. Nobody would think to come looking for me there."

"Good. Give me a week or so and I'll send for you. Go to your mother's house and get what you need. Let her know, I'll be there later on to get

Elijah. Now go!" Aaliyah insisted.

"Okay! I'll see you again soon," Lorita said, hugging her goodbye.

Aaliyah had begun planning her getaway, ever since she fell in love with baby Elijah. Originally she wanted to kidnap Justina's son, to bring her the sort of excruciating pain and heartache she had suffered, after losing her husband and child. Once Aaliyah believed her nemesis had endured enough despair, she planned on returning her son unharmed. But like anything or anyone you take care of for an extended period of time, it's human nature to grow attached. Unfortunately, Aaliyah wasn't prepared for how someone so little and pure would warm her heart. She felt alive again. Loving Elijah filled an empty hole and she never wanted to be without him again.

Chapter 10

Closer To The Truth

"You sounded hysterical on the phone. What's going on?" Amir wanted to know when he let Precious in.

"First, pour me a stiff drink," Precious demanded sitting down on the sofa in the living room. "Thank goodness you answered my call because I can't get in touch with Supreme, Nico or your father. Is Genesis still missing?"

"No, my dad is fine. He was finally able to get rid of Arnez for good but he's having an issue with someone else but he's handling it," Amir explained.

"I'm glad to hear your father is okay but what does that have to do with Supreme and Nico not answering my calls or text messages?"

"They're helping my dad out, along with Lorenzo. Just give them a couple days."

"A couple days?! I don't have a couple days. This is urgent and it can't wait!" Precious barked.

"Calm down," Amir said, taking her glass. She seemed to finish her drink in record time. "Maybe I can help," he offered. "What do you need?"

Precious hesitated before saying fuck it. "Not sure if you heard but Justina's baby was kidnapped."

"Justina had her baby...already? It seems so soon."

"Well she did and now he's gone."

"What fuckin' psycho would kidnap a newborn baby?" Amir shook his head in disbelief.

"It pains me to say this but my own daughter," Precious revealed.

"Aaliyah!? No fuckin' way!" Amir dismissed what Precious said.

"Do you think I want this to be true. I wouldn't be saying it, if I wasn't a hundred percent positive."

"Did you see Aaliyah with the baby or did she admit it?"

"No but…"

"But nothing," Amir interrupted Precious. "Do you realize what you're accusing your own daughter of. Kidnapping is very serious. She could go to jail for years."

"Don't you think I know that, Amir!" Precious shouted. "Why do you think I'm damn near losing my mind right now. Desperate to get in touch with Supreme and Nico. They would be able to talk some sense into her because I ain't gettin' nowhere. All Aaliyah wants to do is deny, deny, deny!"

"Maybe she's denying it, cause it ain't true," Amir barked.

"Obviously, I made a mistake confiding in you," Precious snapped, grabbing her purse. "I need some fuckin' help, not someone who's stuck on stupid."

"Wait!" Amir put his hand up. "Let me go with you and I'll talk to Aaliyah. If you're right and she did take Justina's baby, I believe I can reach her."

"Fine! Let's go."

"But Precious, if you're wrong and I'm right, you need to let this go. Aaliyah has been through enough."

Precious didn't refute what Amir said. She wanted him to be right but deep down she knew he was dead wrong. If going to speak to Aaliyah would allow Amir to accept the truth, then so be it.

"Good afternoon, ladies. Thank you all for joining me today," Angel announced in an inviting tone, looking around the Presidential Suite she reserved to entertain the women There was a fully stocked wet bar, gourmet buffet and anything else they might want to request. "I know many of you are probably wondering why we're having this meeting. There are a few reasons but the first, is reintroducing my former partner, who I'm proud to say is my partner once again, Desmond Blackwell," Angel beamed.

The women clapped their hands, thrilled to see the familiar face. All the ladies adored Desmond, even if sometimes his no nonsense approach to business could be intimidating. They respected him and of course, he was very easy on the eyes.

"Angel, thank you for the very kind introduction and if you don't mind, I'll take it from here."

"Of course." Angel stepped to the side, allowing Desmond to take the lead.

"I'm excited to once again be a part of Angel's Girls. I've always believed in the company and the founder, Angel Blaze. I have several ideas that I'm looking forward to implementing to take our business to the next level. The first is getting rid of every one of you. Your services are no longer needed."

"Wait...what?!" The chatter between the women instantly began.

"Desmond, what are you doing? This isn't what we discussed." Angel objected discreetly.

"Do you want me to be your partner or not?"

"You know that I do but I don't think this is the best way to handle the situation. Without any girls there is no Angel's Girls."

"And without respect you have nothing. Do you trust me?" Angel nodded yes. "Then, let me handle this."

"Continue." Angel moved back, allowing Desmond to finish.

"I'm aware of the disloyalty shown to Angel during my absence. Once someone betrays you, as all of you did, the trust is gone. I cannot do business with people I don't trust."

"I feel I speak for everyone in this room, when I say we all regret betraying Angel," Brittany stood up and said. "That's why when she punished us by not letting us work for a week, we accepted it because we were wrong. So, why are we being punished again?"

"Yeah!" Lexi stood up and chimed in. "It isn't fair." Then Priscilla and the rest of the women stood up, adding their two cents but they were wasting unnecessary time and energy because Desmond's mind was made up.

"Everyone, please have a seat," he politely demanded. He waited for the angry crowd to simmer down before continuing. "Angel chose her punishment and now I'm choosing mine. My decision is nonnegotiable."

"You can't do this! My daughter is about to start preschool. I need my job!" Latrice balked.

"You should've thought about that before you took a job with Juan Martinez. If I recall, Angel was the one who worked around your schedule, when you were trying to find a daycare for your daughter but instead of showing gratitude, you and the rest of these women stabbed her in the back. You won't be rewarded for that...not on my watch."

"Are you going to allow him to do this?" Elsa whispered to Angel. "He's doing too much. It was bad enough business was dead for a week, now this. You need to stop him, Angel," she insisted.

"Desmond, can I speak with you for a moment in private?" Angel walked over to him and asked, as he was finishing up answering questions from the livid group of women.

"In a minute. I'll be right back."

"Where the hell is he going?"

"Elsa, I'm not sure!" Angel cracked. "I'm standing here watching this craziness unfold, the same as you."

This wasn't what Angel had in mind when she asked Desmond to be partners again. It was supposed to be a day of celebrating their alliance but instead the room was filled with chaos.

"I'ma go speak with Desmond and put an end to this. If I allow him to fire all our girls, we mind as well close shop," Angel told Elsa. But before she even headed towards the door, Desmond was back and he brought a gang of bad bitches with him. Each one was prettier than the next but they all looked like they were ready to grace a magazine cover.

"Who are all these women?" Angel was stunned.

"Everyone, these are the new faces of Angel's Girls." Desmond revealed proudly.

"Where did you find them?" Angel's dreadful expression had now lit up with eagerness.

"I got the best of the best women from every city in each state. I told you I had big plans for us. Now do you trust me." Desmond smiled.

"I apologize for ever doubting you. Welcome back, Mr. Desmond Blackwell."

"Are you there?" Justina questioned Shayla who sounded a tad nervous.

"Yeah, I'm inside. Are you sure no one is here? I feel like Elsa lurking around the corner and 'bout to show up saying got you any second."

"Shayla relax. Desmond told me last night, they were having a business meeting at some hotel suite for Angel's Girls and everyone would be there all day. That is why the office is empty and I knew it would be the perfect opportunity for you to do some snooping around," Justina explained, trying to calm Shayla's nerves.

"Well umm, I'm glad you still had a key to the office. It made this the easiest break-in I ever had to do," Shayla popped. "Ooh, Angel left a nice ass diamond bracelet on her desk. I need this in my life!" she said picking it up.

"Put it down!" Justina demanded, as if she could see Shayla trying the bracelet on through the phone. "And make sure you leave it, exactly the way you found it. Are you trying to get busted!"

"Fine!" Shayla huffed. "So what exactly am I looking for?"

"Anything, that has to do with Aaliyah's location, phone number or an address...just anything. I have to go but be thorough, Shayla. I'll call you back in a little bit."

Justina wanted to stay on the phone with Shayla through the duration of her office visit but that changed, when she saw on the security camera, her father was at the door. She knew Shayla could be impulsive and easily get distracted but was hoping the promise of lots of cash, would keep her focused on her task.

"Daddy, hi! You're back. I didn't think I would see you for another few weeks." Justina hugged her father, happy to see him, even though he interrupted something very important to her.

"After I was able to handle some pressing business, I wanted to fly back here and be with you. How's my princess doing today?" T-Roc held his daughter's hand as they sat down on the living room couch.

"I'm doing better."

"You look much better," T-Roc commented seeming surprised.

"Are you saying I looked horrible before?" Justina laughed. "You don't have to answer that. I know I did. I've been trying to take better care of myself. I stopped taking my prescription pills. I'm eating healthier, exercising and getting some sleep. I want to be strong, mentally and physically when my son comes home."

"Have the police gotten some new leads? When we spoke the other the day on the phone, you said there hadn't been any new developments. Has something changed?"

"No, the police are doing the best they can

but I'm feeling more optimistic. I think that has a lot to do with you."

"Me...why me?"

"Because I know you love me and you'll do anything possible to make sure baby Desi comes home."

"You're correct. He's my first and only grandchild and he will come home. Right now, I'm concerned about you." T-Roc squeezed her hand.

"Daddy, like I said, I'm doing much better. I'm trying to become the warrior, you want me to be."

"Are you sure there isn't something you need to tell me?" T-Roc questioned, puzzled by Justina's newfound confidence.

"I told you everything you need to know. Now stop worrying." Justina kissed her father on the cheek. Daughter was more like father, than T-Roc even realized.

Chapter Eleven

In My Feelings

"Obviously Aaliyah's not home," Amir said, after knocking for a couple minutes. Maybe you should call her," he suggested.

"Or maybe, we should just open the door." Precious pulled out a key. "Unbeknownst to my daughter, I had a copy made," she said opening the door.

"Do you ever stop scheming?"

"Not when you have kids to look after." Precious told Amir, when they walked inside Aaliyah's townhouse. "It takes being a parent to understand that logic."

"I'll take your word for it," Amir shot back, looking around. "Who knew Aaliyah was so neat."

"She's not." Precious immediately went upstairs and checked her daughter's drawers and closet. "Fuck!"

"What's wrong?!" Amir ran upstairs.

"Aaliyah's gone. She took all her belongings. Now do you believe me, Amir because innocent people don't run."

"Are you saying you believe Aaliyah ran off with Justina's baby?"

"That's exactly what I'm saying! She knew I was on to her, so she bailed. I'm so stupid!" Precious spit, ready to kick herself.

"What are you talking about?" Amir was baffled.

"For the last few weeks, Aaliyah has been telling me about some mysterious project she was working on and it would require her to leave for an extended period of time. Now I know exactly what that project was, leaving the country with Justina's baby."

"Wow, I guess we know where Aaliyah inherited her scheming skills from," Amir remarked. "What do we do now? Because if what you're saying is true, which I now believe it is, Aaliyah will be spending the best years of her life behind bars."

"I refuse to let that happen. Aaliyah was never the same after the first time she went to jail. Going back will destroy her. I need to find Aaliyah and bring her home before she's too far gone."

"You don't think she already is? I mean she kidnapped another woman's child. That's pretty far gone to me," Amir stated.

"Well, are you too far gone, Amir? Because you basically kidnapped a child too. You just used a fake DNA test to get away with it."

"Damn, that's a pretty low blow, Precious."

"No lower than you writing Aaliyah off, as if she's beyond redemption."

"I didn't meant it that way. All I'm saying…"

"Save it, Amir! The only thing I'm interested in, is finding my daughter and bringing her home. If you're not willing to help me with that, then you can exit to the left, now!" Precious said, going back downstairs.

"Precious wait!" Amir called out.

"I don't have time to wait. I should've never involved you. Just keep what I told you to yourself," Precious snapped. "Supreme and Nico will be able to help me find Aaliyah."

"No they won't." Amir regretted the words coming out his mouth, the moment he said them. But he was trying to get Precious from leaving and it worked.

"What the hell do you mean by that, Amir?" he put his head down, looking away from Precious, which only pissed her off more. "Answer my fuckin' question, Amir!" She screamed, ready to put her heel down his throat."

"I wasn't supposed to say anything but there's a problem involving Supreme, Nico and Lorenzo," Amir reluctantly admitted.

"What kind of problem?"

"It involves some dude named Maverick. He had dealings with Arnez. My dad had him on lockdown at one of the warehouses when he was trying to find Genevieve and Skylar. He told him the location of where they were being held. But before they could have Maverick killed, he got away and now he's seeking revenge."

"Are you saying, he knows Supreme, Nico and Lorenzo helped orchestrate everything?"

"Yes and we think he might have them."

"Dear God, no. Please tell me you're wrong." Precious put her hand over her forehead like she had a migraine. "This can't be happening."

"Precious, we don't know anything for sure, so relax."

"How the fuck am I supposed to relax? You're telling me my husband, Nico and Lorenzo might be dead."

"I didn't say that!" Amir was quick to make clear.

"I've been running these streets, since before you were born!" Precious pointed her finger at Amir's chest. "I know how this fuckin' game work and when muthafuckers come up missing, it ain't because they went on vacation. They either dead or in jail."

"But we ain't talkin' about some regular niggas in the street. Those three men are kings. If anybody can beat the odds in this game, it's them. In the meantime, let me help you find Aaliyah. That's what they would want us to do. Bring her home and keep her out of jail. We need each other to make that happen. Let me help you, Precious," Amir pleaded.

Precious was torn. She wanted to save her

daughter but she was also grieving at the very thought, that three men she had loved at some point in her life, and one that she was married to and deeply in love with, could all be dead. Her nerves were raw but Precious knew what she needed to do.

"Are you sure you have to go out of town?" Desmond asked Justina as she was packing her stuff.

"Yes. I want to go be with my mother for a little while. Being in this house every day, all day without our baby is too much for me right now."

"We can stay at one of our other houses or stay at a hotel suite. We don't have to be here."

"Desmond, I know you love being here because you feel close to our son. I hear you late at night, in his room. It's okay, he'll be home soon."

"But I don't want you to go." Desmond came and held his wife. "I need you here with me."

"Why because I look like the old Justina again, that you fell deeply in lust with," she teased.

"No because you own every piece of my heart and when you leave, it's leaving with you."

"I think that's the sweetest thing you've ever said to me," Justina kissed her husband. "I promise, I won't be gone long but I really need this time with my mother. Please be understanding."

"Okay, just hurry home."

"I will and hopefully our son will be home soon too."

Lorita was in the kitchen, gathering all her favorite snacks, getting ready to watch Ozark on Netflix. She was looking forward to doing some binge watching.

"Trish, hurry up! It's time to watch our show!" Lorita yelled out, getting comfortable on the couch.

"I'm coming. Let me get my chips."

"They're already in here," Lorita said, holding up the bag.

"Damn girl, you brought the whole kitchen in here," Trish cracked.

"Just the good stuff," Lorita laughed, reaching for the remote, ready to hit play. But instead of enjoying the show, Lorita dropped the glass of sprite she was holding. The sound of it crashing on the floor, sounded like an explosion.

"Both of you, get the fuck down!" Two well-built men in army fatigue, brandishing guns stormed through the door and barked.

"What's going on?" Trish cried, her entire body was shaking.

"I don't know. Just do what they say," Lorita muttered, trying not to pee on herself.

"What do you want from us? We don't have any money here but we'll give you what we have," Trish sobbed.

"You! The man pointed his gun at Lorita. "Get up."

"Me?" she asked petrified.

"Who the fuck else got a gun pointed to their head. Now get the fuck up!" The man roared, yanking Lorita's arm.

"Why are you doing this to me...why?!" Tears were streaming down Lorita's face.

"Didn't I tell you to shut up," he said pushing her against the wall. "Where's your phone?"

"Over on the table," Lorita stuttered.

"Both of your phones." The man had a wild glare in his eyes, as if he was looking for a reason to pull the trigger and blow both women away.

"I not sure..."

The man jammed the gun in Lorita's mouth. "You better think long and hard before you say another word. Are you ready to die?"

"Just give him the freakin' phones!" Trish wailed.

Lorita nodded her head, letting the man know she was ready to talk. He removed the gun from her mouth, waiting for her to speak.

"The top drawer in my bedroom."

"Get up and go get it," he ordered, keeping the gun pointed to Lorita's head. He followed behind her as the other man kept his gun on her friend Trish.

"Here it is." Lorita handed the phone to the man.

"Write down your passcodes."

Lorita did what the man asked, confused as to how he knew she had two phones and why he wanted access to them. But if it got both men out of Trish's house, then she would give him whatever he wanted.

"Here," she said, handing him a piece of paper with the information he wanted. After checking to make sure both passcodes worked, he made Lorita sit back down. "I gave you what you wanted. You can leave us alone now."

"Oh, we just gettin' started," the man chuckled, firing multiple bullets in Trish's body. He then walked over and put one directly in her head to make sure she was dead.

Lorita's face was paralyzed from fear. She wanted to scream out in agony, from seeing someone she loved, lying in he own blood but nothing came out. Her childhood friend, who let her come stay at her home, while she waited for Aaliyah to send for her, was dead. And now, Lorita knew she would be next.

Chapter Twelve

In Too Deep

"I still can't believe how Desmond tossed us to the side and brought in them new girls," Riley fumed, puffing on her fifth cigarette. "And to think, I used to have a crush on that nigga."

"Yeah, me too but not no more," Latrice chimed in. "I couldn't even afford to put my daughter in preschool. I got my cousin babysitting while I'm working bullshit jobs," she complained.

"I know what you mean. Lexi back working for that Juan dude but since he know we was all fired and think we desperate, he ain't offering us the same cut, like he was before. Snake ass," Riley scoffed, putting out her cigarette and lighting up another.

"I know, that's why I wasn't fuckin' wit' his ass. But it's hard selling pussy out here, wit' all these crazy muthafuckers. You need to be wit' a legit agency so you don't end up dead," Latrice shook her head. "I should've neva listened to you and fucked over Angel. She always treated us good."

"Oh, so now you wanna blame me! Angel ass didn't even fight for us when Desmond threw us out like yesterday's trash. She ain't no better than him," Riley shouted angrily.

"So, what should we do?" Latrice questioned, always following behind Riley like a lost puppy.

"We won't be pulling in the bread like we were before but I think we should take the gig wit' that Juan dude. But we ain't lettin' Desmond and Angel off the hook. They deserve payback and we gonna give it to them," Riley vowed.

Aaliyah was enjoying her stay with Elijah, at an upscale boutique hotel. They were relaxing on the rooftop by the pool and she loved how peaceful and quiet it was. When Aaliyah decided to leave New York early and relocate, while waiting for all of her paperwork to be complete, she wanted to go someplace that no one would think to look for her. She opted on a small city in the Midwest, Mission Hills, Kansas.

"What a beautiful baby boy you have," a passerby commented, while Aaliyah held Elijah in her arms.

'Thank you so much," she replied sweetly, kissing him on the cheek. As Aaliyah continued to rock him, she noticed she'd missed a text message from her connect in New York. He was letting her know, the paperwork she needed would be ready in a couple days. This was the news Aaliyah had been waiting for. Although she was enjoying the tranquility of Mission Hills, she knew it was time for them to move on.

Aaliyah sent a text to Lorita, letting her know she would be making her airline reservations to join them in Kansas, before jetting off to an unknown destination out of the country. A sense of excitement and sadness came over her. Aaliyah was looking forward to starting a new life with Elijah, where they would be free and no one could take him away from her. At the same time, she knew she'd miss her family. A sense of regret began creeping up on her but she tried to bury those emotions. Aaliyah had come so far with her plan, there was no turning back now.

"If it isn't Fiorella Fuckin' Perez," Justina smiled widely, ripping the tape from over her eyes and mouth. "Or should I call you Lorita, you backstabbing bitch!"

"Justina." Lorita swallowed hard. It was the one face she prayed to never see again but there she was in the flesh.

"That's all you can say? I invited you in my home. Allowed you to take care of my child and you betray me in the cruelest way. I hope conspiring with Aaliyah is worth your life."

"Please let me explain. I had no choice," Lorita managed to say through her terror.

"We always have a choice and you chose to fuck me and my family over royally. Once my men got ahold of your cell phones, I could've easily let them kill you but I didn't. You know why. Because I wanted the pleasure of taking your life myself."

"No! No! Please, don't kill me," Lorita begged. "There has to be a way for me to make this up to you."

"I can't think of one. You literally destroyed my life. I wanted to die the night my son disappeared. I blamed myself. My husband kept asking me, how could I sleep through it all but I had no answers."

"I can give you all the answers you want," Lorita said, determined to stay alive to see another day.

"What kind of answers can you give me, that I can't figure out on my own at this point?"

"Like why you passed out that night. It was me. When I came over that night, before I left, I put a powerful sedative in your tea," Lorita admitted.

Justina thought back to that night and the cup of Tazo Calm Chamomile tea she had to drink, which she routinely did. It didn't even cross her mind it was the reason she passed out.

"I assumed I was just tired," Justina mumbled, realizing she had been blaming herself for no reason. "I could kill you with my bare hands!" Justina lashed out, digging her nails in Lorita's skin, mashing her face.

"Wait! I can answer more questions for you. I can also get your son back!" Lorita screeched, wanting the pain from Justina ripping through her skin to stop.

"I've already seen the text from Aaliyah to you. She's in Kansas. It will take a little bit of time but we'll find her exact location."

"No you won't. Aaliyah is being extra careful, now that her mother knows she's the one who kidnapped your son."

"Are you saying Precious knows Aaliyah has my baby?" Justina wanted to know.

"Yes. She confronted Aaliyah and me but we both denied it. She didn't believe us though. That's why Aaliyah got out of town so quickly. She knew her mother would be back," Lorita spilled.

"Unbelievable! I wonder how many other people know Aaliyah stole my child."

"Aaliyah will never give her exact location through a text message. She will insist on speaking to me on the phone. If not, she'll be suspicious and leave the country with your son."

"She's planning to leave the country with Desi?" Justina became engulfed in fear with the idea of Aaliyah fleeing the country with her baby and never seeing him again.

"Yes. The only reason she's still here is because Aaliyah was waiting for his birth certificate and other paperwork showing she's Elijah's mother, in case there was any legal issues. If she's sending for me, that means it must be ready." Lorita was spilling all the tea in order to stay alive and it was working.

"She changed my son's name from Desmond to Elijah…the nerve of that woman. She has no intention of ever giving me my baby back. Aaliyah better not hurt him!"

"She would never. Aaliyah loves him like he was her own son."

Justina gave Lorita a look of death. She resented her saying how much Aaliyah loved her son but deep down it did give her a sense of relief. Knowing her baby wasn't being hurt or mistreated, eased some of her fears but it didn't make her loathe Aaliyah any less.

"You can help me get my son back but I swear, if you try to fuck me over, I will have you tortured within an inch of your life, before I personally slit your throat," Justina warned.

Angel was on her way to the office when she got a call from a New York number she didn't recognize. "Hello."

"Hi Angel, this is Precious. I hope I didn't catch you at a bad time."

"No of course not. Is everything okay?" Angel asked, since she like never got a call from Precious.

"Yes, everything is fine but I'm having a little difficulty getting in touch with Aaliyah. Have you spoken to her?"

"Actually, I spoke to her a few days ago."

"Really? Did she tell you where she was?"

"She mentioned she'd be doing some traveling and I might not be able to reach her but she'll be in touch. Is something wrong?"

"There's a minor issue regarding Supreme and I wanted to let her know but her cell keeps going straight to voicemail. I was hoping maybe you could be some help," Precious sighed, feeling she had reached another dead end.

"When Aaliyah first called, it was from her cell but we were getting poor reception so she called me back from another number. I think it was a landline. Let me check my recent calls and see if the number is still there," Angel said. There was a brief moment of silence. "Sorry Precious, it's no longer in my phone but I do remember it being a 913 area code."

"Are you sure it was 913?"

"I'm positive. It stuck out to me because I've never gotten a call before from that area code before. I wish I could've been more help."

"Angel, you've been a tremendous help. Thanks so much!"

"You welcome!"

"Oh, and Angel if you hear from Aaliyah before I reach her, don't let her know we spoke. I don't won't her worrying about Supreme."

"Of course. I hope everything works out."

"Me too," Precious said, before hanging up. "Do you know what area code 913 is, Amir?"

"Not off the top of my head but Siri is our friend," Amir joked, instantly getting the answer. "No way, Aaliyah is in Kansas. There's nothing glam girl about that place."

"It's probably the exact reason Aaliyah chose

that place. Call your private investigator and have him check all flights and hotels for the past couple weeks in Kansas and the surrounding area. Angel spoke to her a few days ago, so there's a chance she's still in Kansas," Precious hoped.

"I'm on it."

"Why you're working on that, I have a lead on Lorita. Her mother lives in Queens. I'm waiting for my guy to text me over the address. Once he does, that's our next stop."

Precious wasn't sure what she hated more. Knowing her daughter could spend the rest of her life on the run, or if she got caught, she could spend years in jail. Precious believed there was only one option, find Aaliyah before she ruined her life.

Chapter Thirteen

New Friends And Old Enemies

"Desmond, thank you for seeing me. I wasn't sure you would." Dominique stood in the entryway of his office, in a nervous stance.

"You can come in, Dominique. There's no need to be afraid."

"I'm not afraid. More like anxious. I've been

wanting to call you for weeks now but I wasn't sure if you even wanted to hear my voice," she said, taking a few steps towards Desmond.

"I know we didn't end things on the best of terms but I don't have any ill will towards you, Dominique. I made a decision I felt was best for all of us."

"I get it. You have a wife and child to think about. That was another reason I wanted to see you. I heard your son was kidnapped. I'm so sorry, Desmond. Has there been any change...do you know who has him?"

"Unfortunately, it's a no to both of your questions," Desmond said, closing his desk drawer and walking over to the bar to pour himself a drink. "Can I get you something?" he offered Dominique.

"No, I'm fine. I didn't mean to upset you, asking about your son. I was concerned."

"I appreciate your concern but I don't want to discuss my son with you."

"I understand." She nodded.

"So, how have you've been?"

"I'm doing much better. It was difficult at first, after the accident but I'm finally healed and ready to get back to work."

"It's good to hear."

"Angel was kind enough to offer me a job working with Angel's Girls. But I don't think I would be any good. I only feel comfortable giving my body to a man I love." Dominique fixated her stare on Desmond, with a yearning gaze in her eyes.

"I see." Desmond put down his custom rock glass.

"I really want to dance again. It's my passion."

"I know and you're good at it. I still remember when I walked into that rundown strip club and you stood out like a shining star."

"You saved me, Desmond."

"I did but things have changed. I'm in no position to save you again. It would destroy my marriage and I can't risk that."

"What am I supposed to do. How am I supposed to take care of myself?"

"I'll make some phone calls. I'll get you a job at one of the premier strip clubs but until then, this should hold you over." Desmond pulled out his checkbook.

"I wasn't expecting you to give me money, Desmond."

"I know but I guess writing you a check, eases my guilty conscious. I'm the one who brought you to Miami. It isn't fair I leave you out here without a lifeline. I was angry at you for telling Justina what happened between us but I was wrong for leading you on and cheating on my wife."

"I get you regret what happened between us but I don't. I still love you, Desmond. You're the only man I've ever loved."

"Take this," he said handing Dominique the check. "Now I need for you to go."

"Thank you but…"

"But nothing. Goodbye, Dominique."

Dominique ran out of Desmond's office in tears. She felt embarrassed and humiliated. She envisioned, confessing her undying love to Desmond and he would tell her, the feeling was mutual. Instead, she left feeling rejected and alone. Dominique was so distraught, as tears streamed down her face. She wasn't paying attention to her surroundings and ran smack into someone about to walk through the door.

"I'm so, so sorry!" Dominique cried, in the midst of unraveling. "I didn't mean to bump into you."

"What has a pretty girl like you so upset?"

"Everything. My life is in shambles." Dominique broke down, unable to control the despair she was in.

"Then we need to change that and I believe I can help you. I'm Juan Martinez and you are?"

"Dominique."

"It's a pleasure to meet you, Dominique." He reached out and took her slight hand, placing it in his. Dominique appeared to be like a delicate flower to him. So vulnerable and easily broken, just the way Juan liked his women.

"Can I get another glass of wine?" Lorita stopped the flight attendant as she was walking by.

"Sure, I'll bring it right out."

"Disregard her request," Justina said, leaving the first class section, to sit in the empty seat next to Lorita. "Three glasses of wine is enough."

"You've been counting?"

"Of course. You're no good to me drunk. So get your shit together," Justina demanded.

"I need something to calm my nerves. I had to witness one of my closest friends get killed," Lorita said in a low tone. "And I know if I fuck this up with Aaliyah, then I'm next."

"No one told you to kidnap my baby. So miss me with the pity story. Everything you did, was due to greed. And the only reason you're helping me now, is to save your own life. So yeah, get your nerves in check because if you don't leave that hotel with my son, you're a dead woman. Now buckle up. Our flight is about to land." *Mommy's coming to get you Desi,* Justina said to herself as she closed her eyes.

Aaliyah walked across the custom tile mosaics inset into the gleaming marble floor. She admired the intricately carved wood paneling and playful Renaissance artwork adorning the walls, while also marveling the at the hand-blown Venetian glass chandeliers floating overhead.

"I never thought a small city like Mission Hills, would have such an exquisite hotel," Aaliyah remarked, as she sat in the lobby, waiting for Lorita to arrive.

"Aaliyah hi!" Lorita smiled.

"Hey girl! I was so caught up, playing with this new App I downloaded on my phone, I didn't even see you come in. How are you?" Aaliyah stood up and hugged Lorita.

"I'm good, how are you?"

"Honestly, I'm fantastic!" Aaliyah beamed, sitting back down on the Cascadia blue velvet tufted bench seat. "This town is so peaceful. It's exactly what I needed to relax my mind and prepare myself for this new chapter in my life with Elijah."

"I feel you. Speaking of Elijah, where is he? I've missed the little guy."

"Oh, he's in our hotel suite taking a nap. We had a long day."

"You left him up there alone?"

"Of course not! Don't be stupid." Aaliyah rolled her eyes. "The hotel offers nanny services. Elijah was sleeping so peacefully. I didn't want to wake him, just to come down here and meet you. I'm hungry. They have a great restaurant here," she said grabbing her purse.

"Honestly, I'm pretty tired from the flight. I really wanted to get some rest."

"Well, I already got your room." Aaliyah handed Lorita her room key. "You go rest. I'm going to eat."

"I'll be more than happy to go stay with Elijah while you eat," Lorita offered becoming fidgety.

"I told you, there's a nanny upstairs with him."

"I know but I wanted to see his sweet face."

"I thought you said you wanted to get some rest? And why are you acting so strange?"

"I'm not acting strange. I'm just looking forward to seeing Elijah but I can wait."

"Yeah, you can," Aaliyah sneered. "Now excuse me, I need to eat."

Lorita felt the palms of her hands becoming sweaty. She knew Justina expected her to walk out the hotel with her son but there was no way she could make it happen right now. Lorita wasn't sure if she should go out to the parking lot where Justina and her two goons were and explain the delay, or escape to the hotel room, Aaliyah got for her. At this point it didn't matter, the choice was made for her. Lorita heard a loud commotion and turned to see what was going on.

"I'm going to kill you! You sick bitch!" Lorita heard Justina yell out, as she ran up and tackled Aaliyah like she was a linebacker in the NFL. "You think you can take my son and get away with it! Where is my son!" Justina continued to scream, banging Aaliyah's head against the marble floor. She appeared to be a possessed animal.

"Oh gosh! I have to get outta here!" Lorita raced to a backdoor hotel exit.

Justina was the poster child for an erratic woman so no one dared to come near her. Instead they gathered around and watched as she went postal on Aaliyah, recording with their phones. Luckily, the posh hotel had a police department less than a mile away. They gathered Justina up, quicker than you could say, you're under arrest.

"Get your hands off me! I said get your hands off me!" Justina roared, while trying to break free from the cops so she could wrap her hands around Aaliyah's throat.

"Miss, you better calm down before we taser you," the cop warned. Justina was breathing harder than a bull. But she managed to get her rage in check, allowing the officer to put the handcuffs on and take her to jail.

Chapter Fourteen

I'm Upset

"Where tha fuck you think you goin?" Justina's hired henchman, Cole barked, snatching Lorita up.

"I just needed to get some fresh air," she stuttered.

"And you decide to use the back door. Why not go out the same way you came it? We both know the answer, so no need to say shit," Cole spit, dragging Lorita to the car.

"Are you gonna kill me?"

"Not yet. If you woulda stuck around for a minute, you'd know our boss got arrested. No decisions will be made 'bout yo' life until she gets outta jail."

"It's not my fault she was arrested."

"Did anybody say it was? What is yo' fault, is you didn't come out wit' her baby."

"That wasn't my fault either. Aaliyah left the baby upstairs with a nanny because he was sleeping," Lorita explained.

"Do you know her room number?"

"No but I can go back inside the hotel and try to find out."

"Nah, I ain't takin' no chances wit' you. If you come up missin', our boss won't be pleased. Sam, take us back to the room. We'll wait to see what Justina say, then make our next move."

"I don't need to go to the hospital!" Aaliyah seethed, fighting to get out the ambulance.

"Miss, you were bleeding and unconscious when we arrived at the hotel," the paramedic said. "We have to run test to make sure you don't have any internal injuries."

"Well run the damn test now and let me get the hell out of here!"

"We don't have the proper equipment to run extensive testing. We are the bridge between an emergency and the medical care you'll receive once you get to the doctor. Now please, let us do our job."

"Fine!" Aaliyah reluctantly agreed. She didn't want to bring any additional scrutiny her way because of Elijah. It was only a matter of time before Justina told the cops she kidnapped her son and they came back to the hotel looking for her. The second she could break free, Aaliyah planned to go back to her hotel room, get Elijah and go back in hiding until she could leave the country.

"Justina Blackwell, you're free to go!" Justina walked out her holding cell, angrier than when she went in.

"Daddy, it's so good to see you."

"I got here as soon as I could," T-Roc said, hugging his daughter. "You're a long way from

Miami, Justina. You wouldn't tell me anything on the phone. What happened?"

"I'll tell you when we get in the car. I don't want to talk in here. There's no telling who's listening," Justina huffed, anxious to get the hell out of there.

When they got in the car, Justina only had one thing on her mind. "Drive, daddy. We're going right up the street."

"I'm not driving anywhere until you explain yourself. I mean it Justina. Why were you arrested for felony assault and battery?" T-Roc's incensed tone, made it obvious he wasn't budging.

"I'm here to get Desi."

"Your son...why would he be in Kansas and what does that have to do with your charges?"

"I jumped on Aaliyah in the hotel lobby she's staying at."

"Why would you jump on Aaliyah?"

"Because she's the one who had Desi kidnapped. That treacherous, piece of shit stole my child!"

"Slow down, Justina." T-Roc put his hand on her shoulder. "You have to calm down. "First, are you positive Aaliyah is the one who kidnapped your son?"

"Positive. She was with that nanny I told you about...Fiorella. Her real name is Lorita. She hired her and orchestrated this elaborate scam to steal my child."

"If this is true, why didn't you tell the police?"

"Because I don't want Aaliyah in jail. I want her dead. Now take me to that hotel, so I can get my son and kill her ass!"

"I can't let you kill Aaliyah."

"Why not?!"

"For one, although I don't like Supreme, I have a great deal of respect for him. He wouldn't survive you killing his daughter. And, I wouldn't survive my daughter spending the rest of her life in jail for murder."

"I know how to kill someone and get away with it," Justina mocked.

"After that stunt you pulled in the hotel lobby, with all those witnesses, you'll be the prime suspect if Aaliyah turns up dead. You're thinking with your emotions right now and I get it but killing Aaliyah isn't the answer."

"Then what is because Aaliyah needs to pay for what she's done! I almost lost my mind when Desi was kidnapped." Justina's eyes watered up as she fought to hold back tears. "It felt like my life was over," she started to choke and then Justina couldn't stop bawling.

T-Roc held his daughter closely as she cried on his shoulder. "Baby girl, we'll deal with Aaliyah later. Right now, let's go get your son back."

Chapter Fifteen

Can't Have Everything

"Precious, look who just walked in," Amir said, nudging her arm. She jumped up so quick, he barely had time to put down his drink, so he could catch up to her.

"Aaliyah, how are you and what happened to you?" she questioned, noticing the bandage on her head.

"Mother! What are you and Amir doing here?"

"First, tell me about your head."

"Oh, this," Aaliyah touched the bandage. "It's nothing. I slipped and fell. Now do you want to tell me what brings you all the way to Kansas?"

"You know why we're here," Amir stated. "Don't make this difficult, Aaliyah."

"Is it because I turned my phone off? I mean, I simply wanted some time alone to relax. I apologize for worrying both of you. But as you can see, I'm fine. You can head to the airport and get back to New York." Aaliyah gave her mother and Amir a brief hug. "I'll walk you out."

"Aaliyah, it's over. Cut the shit. We came here to get Justina's baby and we're not leaving until we get him."

"You're back to that again. I don't know what you're talking about. I don't have Justina's baby!"

"Fine," Precious shrugged, taking her phone out her purse.

"What are doing?" Aaliyah questioned.

"Calling the police. I think they should know that a child who has been reported missing in Miami, Florida, is right here in this upscale hotel."

"You wouldn't dare!" Aaliyah snapped, reaching to grab the phone out of her mother's hand.

"Oh, yes the hell I will. If it's the only way to put an end to this foolishness, then so be it. You're not leaving me much of a choice, Aaliyah."

"Yes I am. You and Amir can turn around and leave this hotel and pretend this conversation never happened."

"Aaliyah, come on, don't do this. You don't kidnap babies...you're better than that." Amir tried reasoning with her.

"This coming from the guy who took a baby away from her father, by doing so, put his own sister at risk because you decided to pay someone to switch a DNA test."

"You told her about that?" Amir frowned at Precious.

"Yes she did, so stop acting like you're some saint," Aaliyah snarled at Amir. "Both of you. Mother, you have plenty of skeletons of your own too!"

"Our skeletons change nothing, Aaliyah. Maya kidnapped you when you were a baby, which isn't news to you. That was the scariest time of my life. I will not allow you, to continue to do this to another woman."

"Justina doesn't deserve that beautiful, sweet baby upstairs!" Aaliyah belted.

"You can't play God. It isn't your decision to make."

"What about me and my baby?" she questioned. "Why did God give Justina the perfect child and deny me mine," Aaliyah wept, collapsing in her mother's arms. "It isn't fair. It just isn't fair."

"I know, my sweet child, I know." Precious stroked Aaliyah's hair, allowing her daughter to let it all out. All the pain, anger and sadness she was still holding on to. Instead of healing for the past few months, Aaliyah had been harboring her agony but now she had to let it go.

"Did you get a price on the venue?" Angel questioned Sadie, a new employee. After partnering back up with Desmond, business was beyond booming and the company needed additional help. It was becoming too much for Elsa to handle everything on her own.

"I'm still here. The manager is about to breakdown the different price options."

"Make sure you get full catering and open bar," Angel reminded Sadie.

"Sure thing. I'll call you the moment we're done."

"I'm on my way to a meeting. If I don't hear back from you before I get there, I'll hit you back when I finish. Thanks, Sadie," Angel said ending her call. "Where did I put my car key," she mumbled in frustration, digging through her purse.

Angel was relieved when she located her keys but spazzed out when she saw her car. "Who in the fuck!"

"Damn, someone slashed all yo' tires!" Shayla gasped.

"Was it you? Did you do this shit?!" Angel snapped.

"Girl, you can't be serious," Shayla smacked. "You think I'ma fuck yo' shit up and stay at the crime scene," she said cutting her eyes at Angel.

"Why are you even here?"

"I wanted to see if you had a change of heart about letting me come back to work at Angel's Girls."

"I'm assuming you drove here?"

"Yeah, why?"

"I can't be late for this meeting and I don't have time to wait for a car service."

"Are you asking me," Shayla pointed her stiletto nails against her spaghetti strapped bodysuit. "To take you to your meeting?"

"Yes! Will you take me or not?"

"Sure!" Shayla smiled. "I'm just surprised you didn't take Elsa's car."

"Trust me, I would've but her car is in the shop. Her boyfriend dropped her off to work. Now enough with the questions. Let's go."

"You're the boss." Shayla hurried to her car and unlocked the door for Angel.

"I really do appreciate the ride, Shayla," Angel said, giving her the address.

"Sure you do," Shayla smirked.

"Honestly, I really do. Excuse me for not sounding more enthusiastic but I'm pissed about my car."

"I don't blame you. Expensive ass ride like that. Replacing those tires gon' cost you a pretty penny."

"It's not about the money."

"We all know you a rich bitch," Shayla teased.

"When someone slashes your tires, it's personal."

"True, so who do you have beef wit'?"

"I don't have beef with anybody."

"Well somebody got beef wit' you and you better find out who quick, cause this just the beginning."

"Are you saying this was a message that more is to come?"

"Pretty much. I mean, if I slashed a chick's tires, then I'm probably gon' cut her face up next. Just sayin'," Shayla shrugged, making a right at the light.

"I'll keep that in mind." Angel was mulling over what Shayla said. Slashing her tires was one thing, cutting her face was something else.

"We're here," Shayla announced, turning into the parking lot.

"Great and I'm on time," Angel said, glancing down at her watch. "Thanks again for the ride, Shayla."

"I can wait for you to finish your meeting if you like," Shayla volunteered.

"You don't have to do that. I've already taken up enough of your time."

"I don't mind. I ain't got shit else to do."

"Cool! I shouldn't be in there too long."

"Girl, take yo' time. Like I said, I got all day," she cheesed. Shayla watched Angel head into the office building thinking maybe the ice queen wasn't as cold as she originally thought.

"Hi, I'm here to see Aaliyah Mills. Can you call her room and let her know T-Roc is here to see her?"

"We don't have any guest here by that name," the front desk receptionist informed him.

"Try Clayborn. That's her married name," Justina whispered to her father, pulling down her baseball cap. Due to her recent arrest, Justina was trying to keep a low profile in the hotel.

"I apologize but can you try Aaliyah Clayborn. She recently got married and she might be staying here under her husband's name."

"Of course let me see. Yes, but Mrs. Clayborn has already checked out."

"Are you sure?! She was just here!" Justina yelled, slamming her hands down on the counter.

"I told you to be calm or stay in the car. Are you trying to get arrested again," T-Roc stared down at his daughter.

"Okay." Justina bit down on her lip, so she could restrain herself.

"Thank you for your help," T-Roc said, directing his attention back to the front desk receptionist. "Can you tell me how long ago, Mrs. Clayborn checked out?"

"Sorry sir, but I can't give out that information but I can say she's no longer a guest here at the hotel."

"Thank you. Come on Justina."

"That's it?" Justina spat. "You could've tried harder to get the information from her."

"It would be a waste of time. Besides, we know she hasn't been gone that long."

"It doesn't matter. Aaliyah is probably on a plane right now, headed to who knows where with my son."

"Listen." T-Roc placed his hands firmly on Justina's arms, locking eyes with her. It was vital to him, to reach his daughter. "I'm putting my best men on this. We will find Aaliyah and bring your son home. The good thing is, we know Desmond is safe. You have to trust me."

Justina didn't give her father a verbal response but nodded her head in agreement, which was sufficient enough for T-Roc. He was driving straight to the airport. T-Roc wanted to get them the hell out of Kansas before his daughter got herself in anymore trouble.

"Daddy," she turned to T-Roc. Finally deciding to speak again.

"What is it?"

"I have one more thing to take care of before we leave."

"Which is?"

"The nanny Fiorella, I told you about. I found her. Her real name is Lorita and I brought her here to meet Aaliyah and get my son. She failed, so I had her killed. Cole and Sam, the two men I hired for the job are at a motel on the other side of town. We're in Kansas. They don't know where to dump the body."

"Fuck." He pounded his fist on the steering wheel. "Another mess you've left me to clean up, Justina," T-Roc exhaled, turning the car around.

Chapter Sixteen

Heartbreak Warfare

"How's Aaliyah doing?" Amir asked Precious when she came back downstairs.

"She's resting. Playing all this hide and seek, has drained her, mentally and physically. Sleep is what she needs. How's the little one?" Precious smiled, kissing Desi's hand. "He really is a beautiful baby."

"Yeah, he is. I know Justina must miss him

something terrible," Amir said, cradling the little boy in his arms. "And no I'm not defending Aaliyah but I know this is hard for her too."

"Well don't get too attached because he's going home to his family tomorrow," Precious reminded Amir.

"I know. All I'm saying is, I get why it was difficult for Aaliyah to let him go. I never understood when I would hear people say, babies are a blessing. I get it now. When you hold them, you feel healed."

"Very true. If only they could stay little and sweet like this forever," Precious laughed. "But you're right. This is going to be extremely hard on Aaliyah. It's going to take all of our support to get her through it. I pray to God Supreme, Nico and Lorenzo come back to us soon because Aaliyah will need both of her father's more than ever."

"I agree. How do you think T-Roc is going to react when you bring him Desi tomorrow?"

"Hopefully, he'll be so grateful to have his grandson back, he won't go ballistic on me."

"I think it would be a good idea if you let me come with you," Amir advised. "He's very close to my father and we have a pretty decent relationship too. I can be like a buffer."

Female Hustler Part 6

"Oh gosh, you make me feel like I need to show up strapped," Precious sighed.

"I'm not saying T-Roc is gonna try to kill you but your daughter, did have his daughter's baby kidnapped. It's a given, the tension is gonna be extra thick."

"I get it. I wanted you to stay with Aaliyah but I think she'll be okay by herself for a couple hours. Tomorrow when we go into the city, we'll drop Aaliyah off at her place first, then we'll take Desi to T-Roc. He can make the necessary arrangements, to get the baby back to Justina in Miami."

"Do you think there's a chance Justina is still in Kansas?" Amir questioned.

"I'm sure after she was released from jail, her next stop was back to the hotel. Once Justina found out Aaliyah checked out, I'm sure she couldn't leave Kansas fast enough. And she has no idea where Aaliyah went because we used the private jet. So, I'm sure Justina is back in Miami with her husband."

"I am surprised Justina hasn't gone to the police yet. Having Aaliyah do years behind bars for kidnapping would be the ultimate revenge."

"I have no idea what Justina is thinking. The

important thing is, we have her son and he's safe. I believe that trumps everything. Plus, Aaliyah unfairly, spent all that time in jail because of Chantal and partially because of Justina. T-Roc is a businessman and a father. I'm sure with your help, we can convince him to agree, the slate has now been wiped clean and we can call it even," Precious rationalized.

"Bitch, watch out!" Clarissa gushed when Dominique sat down at their table outside, only steps away from the beach. "That look like some designer shit you wearing," she commented, admiring the two piece rust colored satin set. The short sleeve top had a front tie, highlighting Dominique's taut abs and the wide leg pants, added a touch of sophistication.

"I know absolutely nothing about labels but I'm guessing it's on the pricey side, based on how the material feels and that it compliments my petite figure perfectly," Dominique beamed.

"Girl, you look damn good! Actually you glowing."

"I did have a spa treatment yesterday. I got

a facial and a full body scrub. I feel like a brand new woman."

"You look like one too. That new guy you're seeing, sure knows how to treat a lady. He ain't got a brother...close friend?" Clarissa inquired.

"He has a sister, no brother and I haven't met any of his friends yet but I'll keep a watchful eye."

"Thanks girl. I need a man to swoop in and spoil me. All this sliding up and down the pole gets tiring after a while," Clarissa complained.

"I feel you about the spoiling part. I never knew how nice it was until I met Juan. I mean Desmond treated me good but not in a romantic way. More like he felt pity for me, or obligated. Juan on the other hand, makes me feel special and beautiful," Dominique blushed.

"Because you are."

"Not special or beautiful enough to win Desmond's heart. It belongs to that wicked witch Justina."

"Forget Desmond!" Clarissa popped. "If he don't realize what a gem you are, it's his loss. Girl, you winning. Juan is crazy about you and he's a cutie too."

"But he isn't Desmond."

"I wish I could shake some sense in that

head of yours. I get it. Desmond has the tall, dark and handsome thing going, with a touch of bad boy mystique but he's married now. You need to let it go and move on. You deserve a man who adores you. Don't let Juan slip away because of this obsession with Desmond."

"Maybe you're right. Juan has been patient with me. We haven't even had sex yet."

"You ain't gave that man no pussy and he already spoiling you. Chile, he a keeper. You pulled out all yo' best tricks on Desmond's dick and it got you nowhere. It's time for you to put that energy into Juan. He's earned it."

"Can't argue with that."

"I'm glad you agree. Now let's order some food. I'm famished," Clarissa said, picking up the menu.

Dominique wished she could simply erase Desmond from her mind. After all these months, her feelings hadn't changed at all. She was deeply in love with him, to the point she hoped finally consummating her relationship with Juan, would somehow release the hold Desmond had on her heart.

Female Hustler Part 6

Desmond was in his son's room, standing over the crib he slept in every night until he was taken. This had become a nightly ritual for him. It allowed Desmond to feel connected to his son, although he was far away. Before Desmond got completely lost in his thoughts, he heard the home phone ringing.

"Hello."

"Hey it's me. I tried your cell but you didn't answer," Justina said.

"Baby, it's so good hearing your voice. I left my phone downstairs. That's why I missed your call."

"Let me guess, you're in Desi's room."

"Yep, I am. I thought you would be home by now. I need you here with me. I miss you."

"I miss you more. I really do. I have so much to tell you when I get home."

"I'm in this big house all alone with nothing to do. So, if you wanna tell me now, I have plenty of time to listen."

"I'll wait. I don't want us to discuss heavy stuff right now. I just want to hear your voice and feel your love come through the phone."

"You still didn't tell me when you're coming home," Desmond wanted to know.

"Soon, I promise. I'm helping my father take care of a few things and then I'm coming home to you."

"What things, Justina?"

"Baby, just know, everything I'm doing is for us and our family." Justina then remembered the words her father said to her and repeated them to her husband. "You have to trust me."

Desmond took Justina at her word. He knew the type of woman he married. To him, she was perfectly flawed. If his wife needed more time before coming back home, then Desmond would wait.

Chapter Seventeen

Same Ol' Mistakes

"Good morning, Elsa!" Shayla smiled widely.

"Desiree, that's what's on the schedule for you today. If you have any problems, give me a call back. Bye." When Elsa ended her call, she put an end to her professional tone too. "Damn Shayla, you just keep showing up. Do we need to get a restraining order to keep you out the building. How many different ways do I have to tell you,

you've been fired...let go...don't fuckin' come back." Elsa rose up out her chair and barked.

"Look at you, girl. I ain't know you had all that fire in you. Well excuse me," Shayla laughed.

"Have it your way." Elsa picked up the phone ready to call security.

"There you are!" Angel came out her office and greeted Shayla.

"You're expecting her?" Elsa questioned, hanging up the phone.

"As a matter of fact I am. I'm giving Shayla a trial run as my personal assistant."

"Here you go, Angel. I picked up your clothes from the dry cleaners before I got here," Shayla stated proudly.

"Thank you! Can you just hang them up in my office."

"My pleasure."

"And wait for me in there. I need a moment to speak with Elsa."

"Please tell me this is a joke! You can't seriously be making that nut job your assistant."

"I can hear you!" Shayla called out from the hallway.

"Then go in Angel's office and close the freakin' door!" Elsa shot back.

"I know you don't like Shayla."

"Yeah, I thought that was a mutual feeling we shared."

"It was but I had an opportunity to spend some quality time with Shayla and realized maybe I misjudged her. She deserves a chance to prove herself."

"Not here at Angel's Girls. Get her a job someplace else."

"Elsa, I value you as an employee but that's my name on the front signage of this building not yours. I can hire and fire who I choose."

"Point taken but don't say I didn't warn you."

"It's only a trial run, Elsa. With all the new girls Desmond has brought in, there's really no room on the roster for her right now. She needs a job and I need an assistant. Maybe it will work out, maybe it won't but it can't hurt to give her a try. Now if you excuse me, I have to give Shayla her list of duties for the day."

"Do you," Elsa mumbled under her breath, getting back to work.

I never really talk about the dick that I wanna give you
Or places I wanna get to
Neck grab, head grab
Arch back, heart attack, cardiac
I need it nasty like
Like evil angel, like vivid
You know, nasty like how they give it
You know, I need you to be open like Kay's kitchen
That pussy kinda sound like waves hitting, soothing
Keep it right there, no moving...

Drake's Final Fantasy echoed from the sleek Wisdom Audio LS4s wall speakers in Juan's living room, as Dominique danced seductively to the melodic beat. She was draped in only a provocative blush colored, eyelash lace teddy with strappy back detail and satin trim.

Juan sat with his arms spread across the Bella pearl colored, crescent shape, diamond tufted back sofa, spellbound by how Dominique's body glided towards him. The closer she approached, the harder his dick became.

"Are you ready for me," she whispered to Juan, letting her tongue lick his earlobe.

"I been ready," he replied, sliding the straps of the teddy off Dominique's shoulders. "I want you naked." Juan bit down on her neck, then her breasts until tasting her nipples. Without hesitation, he thrusted every inch inside her wetness, soaking up the juices oozing from her pussy.

Dominique's eyes were closed, allowing every part of her body to relish in how amazing Juan was making her feel. The tingling sensation had her biting down on her bottom lip and digging her nails deep in his back. Juan's sex game was hitting Dominique's g-spot just right but no matter how immaculate it was, the only name she wanted to scream out for, was Desmond.

"T-Roc, can you get the door. I'm going upstairs to bed," Chantal said, pouring herself one more glass of wine before heading up.

"Why so early?"

"Seeing our daughter in so much pain and not being able to do anything about it, has depleted all my energy. Maybe sleep will help me get some of it back," Chantal said, walking up the stairs.

"Whatever works," T-Roc said, opening the door. To his astonishment, there stood Amir and Precious, who was holding his grandson.

"This is a first. T-Roc is speechless." Precious gave him a pleasant smile. "We come in peace. Bringing you and your family the greatest gift you could ever possibly want," she said, placing him in his grandfather's arms. Desi made a high pitched squealing noise, the sound he made when delighted.

"T-Roc, is that baby I hear?" Chantal asked, coming back down the stairs. She stopped when she reached the bottom of the staircase, putting her hand across her chest. For a second, Amir and Precious were scared she was on the verge of having a heart attack. "Dear God, is that my grandson?" her voice cracked.

"Yes, it is?" Amir answered the question, since T-Roc remained mute. This was the very first time Chantal or T-Roc had seen their grandchild in person.

"Please, let me hold him," Chantal said to her husband.

"Not yet," T-Roc spoke up and said. "This is my first time holding my grandson. Just give me a minute." He walked to the living room and sat down in his favorite chair near the fireplace. In the wintertime, T-Roc would seat there with fire burning, drink a glass of cognac while listening to old school classics. He now envisioned having his grandson right by his side during those times. Chantal joined her husband in the living room while Precious and Amir lingered in the back, giving them their moment.

"In a perfect world, they would remain completely in awe of their grandson, to the point it would eliminate all the hatred, I'm sure they have for Aaliyah. But we both know that's wishful thinking," Precious commented to Amir.

"I say let's enjoy the peace and quiet, while we can, cause it ain't gonna last. Get prepared to start groveling," Amir advised.

"I already have and it's about to begin now," Precious said, when T-Roc came walking towards them.

"I want to thank you for bringing my grandson home." Were the first words out of T-Roc's mouth, once he was standing in front of Precious and Amir. "I don't think I've ever seen Chantal this happy in my life," he remarked, glancing back at his wife holding Desi.

"I understand why. You have a very special

grandchild. I only spent a limited time with him and fell in love."

"So did I," Amir added.

"T-Roc, there's no sense in pretending Desi miraculously fell into arms. We're all aware of the role Aaliyah played in his kidnapping but I'm begging you to show my daughter some mercy. Please..."

T-Roc put his hand up. "Stop."

Precious knew his wrath was coming but she hoped T-Roc would at least give her a chance to plead her case, before cutting her off.

"T-Roc, out of respect, can you allow Precious to express herself. This is difficult for her too," Amir stated.

"Thank you, Amir but T-Roc has the right to vent. If I was in his position, I'd be furious too."

"Can you both stop speaking for me and let me talk for myself," T-Roc said, shutting them down before sharing his thoughts. "I don't know what Aaliyah was thinking when she came up with the idea to kidnap Justina's baby. But I've known her since she was a little girl and for her to do something of this magnitude, I know she had to be in tremendous pain. For that reason, I'm going to give your child the forgiveness, you never showed my wife or my daughter, Precious."

"Ouch, that cut deep but I more than deserve the jab. I never did forgive Chantal or Justina and honestly, I never even tried. I guess we're never too old to learn something because if the notorious and ruthless T-Roc can show forgiveness, then I have no excuse for not attempting to do the same," Precious humbly conceded.

"Time will tell if you're being sincere but for now, I'll take your word for it. Now if you excuse me, I'ma go upstairs and wake up Justina and let her know Desi is finally home."

"We had no idea Justina was here. Can I please speak to her before we go?" Precious requested.

"Keep it short, Precious. She hasn't seen her son in weeks."

"I totally understand. I promise I won't take up a lot of her time," Precious assured T-Roc, before he went upstairs.

"Wow, I had no idea Justina would be here," Amir mumbled.

"Why is that a problem for you?"

"Of course not but I haven't seen Justina since we broke up."

"I forgot you still have a thing for her. Well, get over it Amir. Justina has a child with another man and they're married. She's moved on and so should you."

"I'm well aware of that, Precious but it doesn't make it any easier. But I'm a grown man, I can deal," Amir scoffed.

"Chantal, did Justina tell you she was going out?" T-Roc came running down the stairs. Precious could sense a feeling of panic coming from him.

"No, Justina said she was going to bed. She's not in her room?"

"No! I checked everywhere upstairs."

"Unless she took the elevator in the back, without letting us know," Chantal said nervously.

"She's not answering her phone," T-Roc huffed. "Precious, call Aaliyah."

"You think Justina went after Aaliyah?!" Precious became alarmed.

"All I know, is I checked on Justina shortly before you came over and she was in her room resting. Now she's gone," T-Roc said trying to call her again.

"Aaliyah isn't answering her phone either. Damn! Pick up," she mouthed.

"Fuck! Fuck! Fuck!" T-Roc belted.

"Keep your voice down! You're startling the baby," Chantal warned being protective of her grandchild.

"What if Justina woke up and heard you all downstairs. She probably figured Aaliyah came back too," T-Roc rationalized.

"Does Justina know where Aaliyah's townhouse is?" Amir questioned.

"Yes, she does," T-Roc nodded. "Chantal, you stay here with Desi, while I go find Justina."

T-Roc, Precious and Amir rushed out on a mission to locate Justina and Aaliyah. Each of them were praying to find both women unharmed. Given the bad blood between them, they knew it was highly unlikely.

Chapter Eighteen

Worst Behavior

When Justina arrived at Aaliyah's townhouse, she parked directly across the street. Her initial reaction was to run up on the place and use a bat, her gun and foot to kick the door down. After careful consideration, she decided that would bring unwanted attention. So, for the next ten minutes, Justina sat in her car and debated what her next move should be.

I should just go back to my parent's house and be with my son. Precious and Amir brought my baby home safely, that's the most important thing, Justina rationalized. *But I'm sure they're over there right now, begging my dad to forgive Aaliyah and to ask me to do the same, so her trifling ass doesn't go to jail. I'm so sick of her always playing the victim and people giving her a pass, when she's nothing but a self-absorbed, spoiled bitch! If I'd been the one who kidnapped Aaliyah's baby, Precious would be the first person demanding they throw me under the jail, so fuckin' hypocritical!* Justina fumed, getting herself even more worked up.

"Take a deep breath and relax, Justina," she said out loud, trying to calm herself down. She was having flashbacks to everything her father said when he first came to Miami to visit and then when he came to bail her out of jail in Kansas. "Daddy, I want to make you proud, I really do," Justina mumbled, noticing all of his missed calls. She wiped away a tear and decided seeking revenge against Aaliyah wasn't the answer, going home and holding Desi again was. Justina put her foot on the break and was about to hit the start button on her car, when she noticed a familiar face coming around the corner.

"I see you still like taking those nighttime runs, Aaliyah," Justina scoffed, grabbing her gun and throwing her voice of reason, out the window.

Aaliyah was listening to music and felt safe in her quiet treelined neighborhood. The run was exactly what she needed, to take her mind off all that went wrong in the last forty-eight hours. She reached in a small compartment in the waistband of her running leggings to get her key.

Justina had quietly snuck up behind an unsuspecting Aaliyah. Making sure to wait until she actually unlocked the door before making her move. Like a cat prowling in the night, Justina attacked her prey the moment the door opened. She leaped on top of Aaliyah's back, using the weight of her body to keep her face pressed to the floor.

"Get ready to die!" Justina roared, pressing the barrel of her gun against Aaliyah's head. "You stole my son and really thought you'd get away with it. The joke is on you!"

"Justina, my mother and Amir are bringing your son home as we speak. Elijah might already be at your parent's house right now," Aaliyah said, gasping for air.

"His name is Desi! He was named after his father Desmond Blackwell not fuckin' Elijah, you sick fuck!" Justina screamed, knocking Aaliyah in the back of the head with her gun.

Aaliyah yelled out in pain. She could feel an open gash in her head and the warm blood dripping down, mixing with the sweat on her face. "You're right...I'm sorry," Aaliyah managed to say through her pain.

"You always talked about how sick and crazy my mother was and that I was just like her but what's your excuse, Aaliyah? What type of woman steals another woman's baby? Explain that to me. You even got a fake birth certificate, listing you as his mother! I guess I should've just handed you my husband too, then you can take over my whole fuckin' life. You're pathetic! I'm sure Dale's turning in his grave right now!"

That last comment from her nemesis, sent Aaliyah reeling. She swung her arm wildly, hitting Justina in her ear. Caught up in her own rage, spewing her frustrations, made Justina completely unprepared when Aaliyah decided to strike back. She swung on Justina again, this time knocking the gun out her hand.

Justina leaped to the floor, trying to retrieve

the weapon but Aaliyah grabbed her leg, pulling her back towards her.

"Get off me!" Justina yelled, stomping her Nike shoe to hit Aaliyah in the face but instead, Aaliyah let her leg go and made her own go for the gun. Both women struggled to stand up, so they crawled but Aaliyah was winning the race which prompted Justina to grab Aaliyah's ponytail to slow her down, only pissing Aaliyah off more.

"You wanna fuck with me! Watch me end you!" Aaliyah balled up her fist, landing a right hook across Justina's cheek. The powerful punch caused her to fall back and Aaliyah took full advantage. She jumped on top of her former best friend and started choking her. Aaliyah was blinded by rage, watching the life drain from her face.

But Justina wasn't ready to surrender to defeat. She tried digging her nails into Aaliyah's eyes, making her loosen the grip around Justina's throat. Justina coughed profusely but also regained enough strength to land her own punch across Aaliyah's nose. When she reached up to dab the blood coming from her nose, Justina pushed her off and stood up.

"I'm not done with you!" Aaliyah jumped

up and swung on Justina and she swung right back. The women continued exchanging blows. They were both bruised, battered and tired ass fuck. But the mutual hatred they shared for one another, kept their adrenaline pumping. Aaliyah and Justina were willing to fight to the death of them.

"Based on the size of those diamond studs in your ears, I'm guessing the romantic evening you planned for Juan the other night was a success," Clarissa cracked, getting comfortable on the couch with her glass of wine.

'That would be a yes. Juan is like the boyfriend you always dreamed of having but thought only existed in the movies. He makes me feel like a princess," Dominique giggled.

"Wait! Did I hear you correctly. You called Juan your boyfriend?"

"I guess I did, didn't I," she smiled. He kinda made it official when we woke up the next morning."

"I'm all for fast tracking a relationship but this is on some super speedy shit. You ready for that? I mean, just last week you were pining over Desmond. Your new boyfriend doesn't mind sharing your heart with another man?" Clarissa sulked.

"I didn't tell Juan about Desmond. I told you, when I first met him, he was going inside the club. He never told me why but I'm thinking they might be in the same line of work. Plus, it doesn't even matter. Desmond was never my man and it ain't like he would ever claim me," Dominique shrugged.

"Girl, just be careful. Most men don't take kindly to spoiling a chick who sprung on another nigga."

"Listen, I've given up on this fantasy of Desmond realizing I'm the right woman for him and not that snob he married Justina." Dominique pouted. "It might take some time but I think eventually, Juan will make me forget all about my one sided obsession with Desmond. I'm gonna give the relationship my all. Like you said, Juan is a great catch. I can't let someone else swoop in and steal him away," Dominique winked, raising her wine glass.

Clarissa joined Dominique in raising her glass, "Cheers to that!"

"I booked your flight and reserved car service for you but you know I don't have no problem dropping you off. Just say the word, Angel."

"I know Shayla, but it's super early in the morning. No sense in you waking up at the crack of dawn."

"Cool. Also, when I made your hotel reservations, I insisted they give you a water view. Let me know if they don't because I wrote down the agent's first and last name, who promised, to make sure you were properly accommodated," Shayla smacked.

"I will definitely let you know," Angel laughed. "I never imagined seeing you sitting in my office, holding a day planner and a pen, taking notes. You seem to be taking your new position as my personal assistant very seriously."

"I am! You've given me an opportunity to prove myself. Real talk, I'm glad there wasn't no availability to come back as one of Angel's Girls. Excuse my language for as second boss," Shayla put her hand up. "Although the money is good, selling pussy takes a toll on you."

"I'm sure it does," Angel nodded. "That's why I try to accommodate my girl's, as much as one can, in a business like this. I know you can easily get burnt out but like you said, the money is good. A lot of the girls get addicted to the fast cash and refuse to give it up."

"I might not be rolling in the dough being your personal assistant but the perks have been nice and for the first time, I feel proud of myself. I don't mind telling people what I do. And I know, you haven't decided if this will be a permanent position for me but for the time being, I'm enjoying myself."

"I'm glad to hear that, Shayla. Keep up the good work and the position will turn permanent before you know it. Now, you can have the rest of the day off."

"Are you sure?"

"Yes! I need to pack for my trip in the morning and I want to spend some quality time with my hubby before I leave," Angel smiled.

"Sounds like fun. Get home to that fine man of yours and if you change your mind and want me to pick you up from the airport when you get back, let me know."

"Will do and try to have some fun today.

You've earned it cause you been working yo' ass off!" Angel beamed.

"Girl, I think I will... bye boss," Shayla waved.

When Shayla got in her car, she lit up a smoke and made a phone call.

"Aren't you supposed to be working?"

"My boss gave me the rest of the day off. She also insisted that I have some fun. So, you know I had to call you," Shayla smirked.

"Lucky for you, I'm working from home today. Bring yo' sexy ass over here."

"On the way."

It seemed by the time Shayla ended the call and finished her smoke, she was butt naked in bed, straddling Juan. "Damn, I missed this dick," she moaned, riding him while he snorted coke off her tits.

Fucking and snorting coke was just two of the things Shayla and Juan had in common. They probably would've never crossed paths if it wasn't for her now deceased cousin Taren. She had dealings with a few unsavory men in Mexico. Running credit scams and of course trafficking drugs. Taren wasn't heavy on the drug scene but when she wanted to make some quick cash, she was more than willing to provide her assistance. When Juan showed up one day at her crib, looking for her cousin, a conversation about Taren's death, turned into Shayla being bent over on the table, getting dug out by Juan.

Soon their routine sex sessions and dabbling in coke, led to pillow talk. They learned they shared more than just their lust for sex and drugs. Juan had a hard on for Desmond and Shayla loathed Angel. Juan was trying to infiltrate Desmond's business operations and figured starting with Angel's Girls would be the easiest way. But when Shayla got fired, she had to find another way in. It wasn't until Justina hired her to break into their office building to get contact information on Aaliyah, did the bright idea of becoming Angel's assistant kick in. Her office was unorganized and disarray. In her opinion the girl needed help. It was Juan who orchestrated the business meeting for Angel and had her tires slashed, all Shayla had to do was be at the right place at the right time.

"Angel told me to have some fun today and you delivered, like you always do, papi." Shayla said, reaching for a cigarette as she laid in bed with Juan.

"You think she's warming up to you?"

"Hell yeah! That stuck up bitch love me kissin' her ass. She feel like she doin' charity work, fuckin' wit' me," Shayla laughed. "How are things goin' wit' you and olé' girl?"

"Coming along. I got her right where I want her," Juan stated with coolness.

"Taren said that hoe was slow but be careful. Because my cousin also said, Dominique was real good at playing the damsel in distress role."

"I already figured that out. She still hasn't even told me about her dealings with Desmond."

"I guess she don't want to hurt yo' feelings," Shayla teased. "Cause I already told you, Taren said she had it bad for that nigga."

Juan listened to what Shayla had to say but she wasn't telling him anything he didn't already know. He was seasoned in the area of reading people and it was obvious to him, someone had hurt Dominique something terrible. Lavishing her with pricey gifts was simply a shortcut Juan took, to break down the walls she'd put up. At first, he wasn't sure it was having the effect he intended. But once Dominique gave up the pussy,

Juan knew, he'd gotten inside her head.

"No more talking," Juan said, taking one more snort of coke off the glass nightstand. "I'm ready to fuck some more."

Shayla decided to have even more fun and sprinkled some coke on Juan's thick dick. She pressed down on her nostril, snorting up the nose candy, before giving him the ultimate blow job, guaranteeing they would be fucking all day and night.

Chapter Nineteen

Game Over...
A New One Begins

"The front door is wide open! Oh gosh, this isn't good!" Precious cried out in fear, when T-Roc pulled up. He didn't even bother parking. He quickly turned off the car, put on the emergency lights and they all jumped out, running towards Aaliyah's place.

"I pray we're not too late." Amir said under his breath, thinking the worst but hoping for the best.

"Justina!"

"Aaliyah!"

T-Roc and Precious shouted their daughter's names simultaneously. What they witnessed broke their hearts. Aaliyah and Justina both looked like they had gone twelve rounds with professional boxers. Only their fury for each other, fueled them with enough energy to remain standing.

"Daddy, you need to go," Justina shouted, keeping her gun aimed at Aaliyah.

"Justina, what are you doing? We talked about this," T-Roc spoke with great sadness in his voice.

"Aaliyah, are you okay?" Precious asked, stepping forward.

"Get back or I'll put a bullet in her!" Justina shouted.

"Mother, I'm fine," Aaliyah said, too exhausted to say much more.

"Put down the gun, Justina. You don't want to do this," T-Roc stressed to her.

"But I do. She deserves it. She had Lorita

drug me, steal my son and was planning to leave the country with him. I almost lost my mind because of this piece of shit!" Justina spit on the floor where Aaliyah stood. "She doesn't deserve to live!"

"Justina, you might be right but what about your beautiful son?" Amir came closer, showing his face.

"Stay out of this, Amir! This has nothing to do with you."

"But it does. Just because we're not together anymore, doesn't mean I don't still care about you. You have too much to live for. Don't throw your life away like this," Amir pressed.

"Just shut up! All of you! This is between me and Aaliyah! Just go! All of you just go!" Justina screamed, tightening her grip on the trigger.

"We're not going anywhere. If you kill Aaliyah, you will have to do in front of all of us, including me." T-Roc made clear. "Is that what you want your father to see. His only daughter, killing another human being?"

"Daddy stop!"

"You have a beautiful son, waiting to be reunited with his mother but you're willing to throw it all away and spend the rest of your life in prison, for murder. That makes what you're doing, no better than what Aaliyah did."

Those words resonated deeply with Justina. Flashes of seeing little Desi coming to see her behind bars, made her sick to her stomach. For the first time, since regaining the upper hand in their fight to the death, Justina relaxed her stance and Aaliyah wasn't taking any chances with her life. She leaped forward, trying to yank the gun away from her adversary. The women struggled with the gun and then silence filled the room, when a shot was fired.

The room seemed to be frozen. No one was sure what happened, until T-Roc lifted his hand and there was blood covering his shirt. Justina immediately released her hand off the gun and ran to her father.

"Daddy! Daddy! I'm so, so sorry. This is all my fault!" Justina cried.

"It's okay," T-Roc said calmly, sitting down on a chair. I just took a bullet in the shoulder," he explained, immediately applying pressure.

"Come on, let's get you fixed up," Amir said, helping T-Roc. "Precious, will you and Aaliyah be okay? I'ma take T-Roc to get his gunshot wound taken care of."

"We're fine," they both nodded. "You go ahead. Let me know how everything goes," Precious said, hugging onto her daughter.

"T-Roc, I'm sorry," Aaliyah called out, as he walked past her, with Justina holding his hand. He simply nodded his head, without saying a word.

"Are you sure you're okay?" Precious asked Aaliyah again, after everyone left.

"I'm fine. I'm not the one who left here with a bullet," Aaliyah huffed, going into the kitchen to get a bottle of water. "Can I get you something?"

"I don't think what you have, is strong enough for what I need," Precious sighed. "This whole ordeal has been a complete nightmare but what's scarier is, it could've ended up a lot worst."

"Who you telling. I really believed Justina was gonna kill me. She had so much hate in her eyes."

"Can you really blame her, Aaliyah?"

"Are you seriously defending her?!" Aaliyah shouted. "She almost killed me!" she spit with indignation.

"I'm not defending Justina but you're not innocent in this either. You had her son kidnapped."

"And I also gave him back."

"Not voluntarily," Precious reminded her headstrong daughter.

"Whatever," Aaliyah shrugged. "Justina can now go back to her perfect life, with her beautiful son and husband. Since she couldn't kill me, I'm sure she's plotting right now, to turn me in to the police on kidnapping charges. Instead of a grave, I guess a jail cell will have to suffice," she spewed her eyes.

"This rivalry between you and Justina has to end. It's one thing to take her boyfriend, Aaliyah, it's another to take her child. There's no reason for you all to be in competition with each other," Precious emphasized to Aaliyah.

"You're absolutely right because there is no competition. Justina is still the same insecure, plain jane girl, wearing glasses, she was when we were growing up. Because she learned to put on some makeup, do her hair and wear sexy clothes, doesn't change who she is deep down inside," Aaliyah scoffed.

"The point is, we all need to start healing, especially you, Aaliyah."

"I can't do that if I'm locked up!"

"T-Roc promised he would make sure you wouldn't spend one day in jail," Precious asserted.

"As if he has any control over that neurotic daughter of his."

"Well, he was able to talk her down from shooting you. He has more influence over Justina then you might think."

"Maybe but I don't trust anyone in that family, including T-Roc."

"Aaliyah, let's not think about any of that right now. I'm emotionally drained and I'm sure you are too. Right now, you should rest."

"I agree. I'm going upstairs to take a long hot bath."

"Sounds like a good idea, sweetheart."

"And mom," Aaliyah stopped herself before going upstairs. "Thank you. You always come through for me. I don't know what I would do without you," she said, giving Precious a hug and kiss.

Precious laid back on the couch and closed her eyes after Aaliyah went upstairs. She loved her daughter more than anything. After everything they went through today and surviving it, instead of feeling relieved, she was flooded with worry. It concerned her that instead of seeming remorseful for what happened, Aaliyah was angry. Precious was determined to figure out a way to help her daughter to start healing, no matter what she had to do.

"So, that's the entire story, from beginning to end." Justina stated, sitting on the armchair smiling at her husband and their son.

"And quite a story it is," Desmond said, shaking his head. "I still wish you would've come to me. I should've been there to help you. Dealing with all that craziness by yourself, it angers me."

"Baby, it all worked out and my father was amazing. Honestly, this whole ordeal brought us closer together. I hate this had to happen," Justina said, stroking Desi's hair. "But I truly understand the importance of family now. I love you so much, Desmond. Now more than ever."

"I love you too." He leaned up to kiss his wife.

"You and Desi are my world and nothing will ever tear us apart," Justina swore. "Baby, you stay here with little Desi and I'll get the door," she said getting up.

"Good afternoon, Justina."

"Amir, what are you doing here? If you're coming to check up on me, I'm fine."

"I'm glad to hear that. Can I come in?"

"Of course." Justina stepped to the side, allowing Amir inside. "You still haven't told me why you're here," she said, closing the door.

Amir stared over at Desmond who was holding Desi in his arms. He glanced back at Justina before resting his eyes on her husband. "I came here to get my son and I'm not leaving until I do," Amir vowed.

A KING PRODUCTION

Rich or Famous
Rich Because You Can Buy Fame

A NOVEL

JOY DEJA KING

Welcome To My World

✶✶★✶✶

Before I die, if you don't remember anything else I ever taught you, know this. A man will be judged, not on what he has but how much of it. So you find a way to make money and when you think you've made enough, make some more, because you'll need it to survive in this cruel world. Money will be the only thing to save you. As I sat across from Darnell those words my father said to me on his deathbed played in my head.

"Yo, Lorenzo, are you listening to me, did you hear anything I said?"

"I heard everything you said. The problem for you is I don't give a fuck." I responded, giving a casual shoulder shrug as I rested my thumb under my chin with my index finger above my mouth.

"What you mean, you don't give a fuck? We been doing business for over three years now and that's the best you got for me?"

"Here's the thing, Darnell, I got informants all over these streets. As a matter of fact that broad you've had in your back pocket for the last few weeks is one of them."

"I don't understand what you saying," Darnell said swallowing hard. He tried to keep the tone of his voice calm, but his body composure was speaking something different.

"Alexus, has earned every dollar I've paid her to fuck wit' yo' blood suckin' ass. You a fake fuck wit' no fangs. You wanna play wit' my 100 g's like you at the casino. That's a real dummy move, Darnell." I could see the sweat beads gathering, resting in the creases of Darnell's forehead.

"Lorenzo, man, I don't know what that bitch told you but none of it is true! I swear 'bout four niggas ran up in my crib last night and took all my shit. Now that I think about it, that trifling ho Alexus probably had me set up! She fucked us both over!"

I shook my head for a few seconds not believing this muthafucker was saying that shit with a straight face. "I thought you said it was two niggas that ran up in your crib now that shit done doubled. Next thing you gon' spit is that all of Marcy projects was in on the stickup."

"Man, I can get your money. I can have it to you first thing tomorrow. I swear!"

"The thing is I need my money right now." I casually stood up from my seat and walked towards Darnell who now looked like he had been dipped in water. Watching him fall apart in front of my eyes made up for the fact that I would never get back a dime of the money he owed me.

"Zo, you so paid, this shit ain't gon' even faze you. All I'm asking for is less than twenty-four hours. You can at least give me that," Darnell pleaded.

"See, that's your first mistake, counting my pockets. My money is *my* money, so yes this shit do faze me."

"I didn't mean it like that. I wasn't tryna disrespect you. By this time tomorrow you will have your money and we can put this shit behind us." Darnell's eyes darted around in every direction instead of looking directly at me. A good liar, he was not.

"Since you were robbed of the money you owe me and the rest of my drugs, how you gon' get me my dough? I mean the way you tell it, they didn't leave you wit' nothin' but yo' dirty draws."

"I'll work it out. Don't even stress yourself, I got you, man."

"What you saying is that the nigga you so called aligned yourself with, by using my money and my product, is going to hand it back over to you?"

"Zo, what you talking 'bout? I ain't aligned myself wit' nobody. That slaw ass bitch Alexus feeding you lies."

"No, that's you feeding me lies. Why don't you admit you no longer wanted to work for me? You felt you was big shit and could be your own boss. So you used my money and product to buy your way in with this other nigga to step in my territory. But you ain't no boss you a poser. And your need to perpetrate a fraud is going to cost you your life."

"Lorenzo, don't do this man! This is all a big misunderstanding. I swear on my daughter I will have your money tomorrow. Fuck, if you let me leave right now I'll have that shit to you tonight!" I listened to Darnell stutter his words.

My men, who had been patiently waiting in each corner of the warehouse, dressed in all black, loaded with nothing but artillery, stepped out of the darkness ready to obliterate the enemy I had once considered my best worker. Darnell's eyes widened as he witnessed the men who had saved and protected him on numerous occasions, as he dealt with the vultures he encountered in the street life, now ready to end his.

"Don't do this, Zo! Pleeease," Darnell was now on his knees begging.

"Damn, nigga, you already a thief and a backstabber. Don't add, going out crying like a bitch to that too. Man the fuck up. At least take this bullet like a soldier."

"I'm sorry, Zo. Please don't do this. I gotta daughter that need me. Pleeease man, I'll do anything. Just don't kill me." The tears were pouring down Darnell's face and instead of softening me up it just made me even more pissed at his punk ass.

"Save your fuckin' tears. You shoulda thought about your daughter before you stole from me. You're the worse sort of thief. I invite you into my home, I make you a part of my family and you steal from me, you plot against me. Your daughter doesn't need you. You have nothing to teach her."

My men each pulled out their gat ready to attack and I put my hand up motioning them to stop. For the first time since Darnell arrived, a calm gaze spread across his face.

"I knew you didn't have the heart to let them kill me, Zo. We've been through so much together. I mean you Tania's God Father. We bigger than this and we will get through it," Darnell said, halfway smiling as he began getting off his knees and standing up.

"You're right, I don't have the heart to let them kill you, I'ma do that shit myself." Darnell didn't even have a chance to let what I said resonate with him because I just sprayed that muthafucker like the piece of shit he was. "Clean this shit up," I said, stepping over Darnell's bullet ridden body as I made my exit.

Read The Entire Bitch Series in This Order

P.O. Box 912
Collierville, TN 38027

A KING PRODUCTION

www.joydejaking.com
www.twitter.com/joydejaking

ORDER FORM

Name:
Address:
City/State:
Zip:

QUANTITY	TITLES	PRICE	TOTAL
	Bitch	$15.00	
	Bitch Reloaded	$15.00	
	The Bitch Is Back	$15.00	
	Queen Bitch	$15.00	
	Last Bitch Standing	$15.00	
	Superstar	$15.00	
	Ride Wit' Me	$12.00	
	Ride Wit' Me Part 2	$15.00	
	Stackin' Paper	$15.00	
	Trife Life To Lavish	$15.00	
	Trife Life To Lavish II	$15.00	
	Stackin' Paper II	$15.00	
	Rich or Famous	$15.00	
	Rich or Famous Part 2	$15.00	
	Rich or Famous Part 3	$15.00	
	Bitch A New Beginning	$15.00	
	Mafia Princess Part 1	$15.00	
	Mafia Princess Part 2	$15.00	
	Mafia Princess Part 3	$15.00	
	Mafia Princess Part 4	$15.00	
	Mafia Princess Part 5	$15.00	
	Boss Bitch	$15.00	
	Baller Bitches Vol. 1	$15.00	
	Baller Bitches Vol. 2	$15.00	
	Baller Bitches Vol. 3	$15.00	
	Bad Bitch	$15.00	
	Still The Baddest Bitch	$15.00	
	Power	$15.00	
	Power Part 2	$15.00	
	Drake	$15.00	
	Drake Part 2	$15.00	
	Female Hustler	$15.00	
	Female Hustler Part 2	$15.00	
	Female Hustler Part 3	$15.00	
	Female Hustler Part 4	$15.00	
	Female Hustler Part 5	$15.00	
	Female Hustler Part 6	$15.00	
	Princess Fever "Birthday Bash"	$6.00	
	Nico Carter The Men Of The Bitch Series	$15.00	
	Bitch The Beginning Of The End	$15.00	
	Supreme...Men Of The Bitch Series	$15.00	
	Bitch The Final Chapter	$15.00	
	Stackin' Paper III	$15.00	
	Men Of The Bitch Series And The Women Who Love Them	$15.00	
	Coke Like The 80s	$15.00	
	Baller Bitches The Reunion Vol. 4	$15.00	
	Stackin' Paper IV	$15.00	
	The Legacy	$15.00	
	Lovin' Thy Enemy	$15.00	
	Stackin' Paper V	$15.00	
	The Legacy Part 2	$15.00	
	Assassins - Episode 1	$11.00	
	Assassins - Episode 2	$11.00	
	Assassins - Episode 3	$11.00	
	Bitch Chronicles	$40.00	
	So Hood So Rich	$15.00	
	Stackin' Paper VI	$15.00	
	Female Hustler Part 7	$15.00	
	Toxic...	$6.00	

Shipping/Handling (Via Priority Mail) $8.95 1-3 Books, $16.25 4-7 Books. For 7 or more $21.50.
Total: $_____ FORMS OF ACCEPTED PAYMENTS: Certified or government issued checks and money Orders, all mail in orders take 5-7 Business days to be delivered

www.ingramcontent.com/pod-product-compliance
Lightning Source LLC
Chambersburg PA
CBHW030150100526
44592CB00009B/205